TEACH YOUR CHILD BRIDGE

using a simplified Acol system

RON KLINGER

LONDON
VICTOR GOLLANCZ LTD
in association with
PETER CRAWLEY
1990

First published in Great Britain 1990
in association with Peter Crawley
by Victor Gollancz Ltd
14 Henrietta Street, London WC2E 8QJ

British Library Cataloguing in Publication Data
Klinger, Ron
Teach your child bridge. – (Master bridge series).
1. Contract bridge. Acol bidding
I. Title II. Series
795.41'52

ISBN 0-575-04737-2

Photoset and printed by WBC Print Ltd, Bristol

Contents

by Ron Klinger

GUIDE TO BETTER ACOL BRIDGE
PLAYING TO WIN AT BRIDGE
100 WINNING BRIDGE TIPS
THE MODERN LOSING TRICK COUNT
IMPROVE YOUR BRIDGE MEMORY
WORLD CHAMPIONSHIP PAIRS BRIDGE
BRIDGE WITHOUT ERROR
ACOL BRIDGE MADE EASY
BASIC BRIDGE
BASIC ACOL BRIDGE FLIPPER
ACOL BRIDGE FLIPPER
DUPLICATE BRIDGE FLIPPER
FIVE-CARD MAJORS BIDDING FLIPPER
MASTER OPENING LEADS
MASTER PLAY AT TRICK 1
MASTER DOUBLES
MASTER CUE BIDDING TO SLAMS

Introduction

There is almost no lowest age at which children can enjoy the pleasures of card play. Bridge is generally considered the most complex and difficult of card games, yet there is no reason why children cannot play, even though the intricacies and brilliancies may elude them at the start (just as they tend to elude all beginners).

This book provides an easy and comfortable path for children to come to grips with bridge. From the tenderest years to the late teens, there are plentiful games to provide a challenge and grip the imagination. This is not a course of lessons. There is no time limit in which the book must be completed. The aim of the book is to stimulate the child, to provide the background for children actually to play bridge, to have fun. There is no pressure to study and absorb sophisticated methods, systems or conventions.

The book is divided into two sections. The first covers a host of card games which have been designed to incorporate bridge principles. They are graded by ages and degree of difficulty and you will need to gauge whether your child is able to manage the next series of games. By playing these games you will enable the child to acquire 'card sense'. Many of the games are intriguing in themselves and good fun for adults, too. You may find yourself introducing some to your bridge cronies.

Section 2 covers a very basic approach to bidding based on the Acol system. If you already play bridge, you will know Acol already or have no trouble learning the system. If you are not yet a bridge player, this provides a painless start to bidding. Acol is the most common and most popular system throughout Great Britain and much of Europe.

This section will enable a child (or an adult) to learn to value a hand and bid competently in a very short time. Acol is a natural system, logical, easy to follow and based on the principle of 'Bid what you think you can make'. One huge advantage is that it will allow you to play bridge with children without hours and hours of study.

In all bridge partnerships, it is important that you both play the same system. Even if you are already a competent player, make sure you peruse the material from Chapters 7 onwards so that you are both using the same methods. By learning it together, you will know what the child knows.

A word of warning: Do not impose or encourage the child to use other methods, ones that you might prefer, while the child is just starting. At this stage it is best to keep it as simple as possible, to avoid exceptions to basic approaches and generally to ignore mistakes. Make it simple, make it fun, leave additional learning till later. It is also best in the early stages to play only against other players using the same methods. As Acol is so widely played, this is no problem.

If you succeed in arousing an enthusiasm for bridge without dwelling on its complications, you will be surprised at how quickly the child will want to know more, to improve bidding and play techniques. At that stage it will be time to move on to another book dealing with more advanced areas of bidding or with card play (or both).

Although this book has been written to enable children to play bridge, there is another group which can benefit from it. The working spouse is often under considerable pressure to play bridge but the usual excuses are 'I don't have the time' or 'There's too much to learn'. If you would like your spouse to take a greater interest in bridge, the basic Acol system may be the answer. There is not much learning, the principles are simple and it takes little time to absorb. To be able to play a competent game is an asset socially and in business. Do not be surprised if you soon have a new bridge addict on your hands.

Ron Klinger 1990

Chapter 1

Introducing Bridge To Your Child

One of the most amazing features about bridge is that it is a game for young and old alike. Players into their nineties are still fascinated and have won club championships. Players in their eighties have won national titles and players in their seventies have represented their country and have won world championships.

Yet the young have just as much claim to fame. Players in their teens have won national championships and players in their twenties have won world championships, both in the open and the women's divisions. In the U.S.A., children of 11 have become Life Masters, a status that eludes the majority of the world's players. It is truly an incredible phenomenon that a game can span the generations in this manner.

Another amazing aspect is that there is almost no age too young to start bridge. If it were suggested children should not start before the age of 6, a flood of anecdotes would pour in, confirming that children of 5 were managing quite well, thank you. If a limit of 5 were set, four-year-olds would soon be reported as playing an adequate game.

Just as each child is different, so a suitable age at which to start bridge will be different. There is no *right* age but there is a *right* approach. In addition, there are certain factors by which you can judge a child's readiness to start on bridge.

(1) Competence at arithmetic addition:
In the early stages, there is a lot of point counting, adding up the points in your hand, adding partner's points to your own, and so on. Children tend to become facile with numbers between the ages of 5 and 10. When such competence becomes obvious, one important criterion for starting bridge is present. It would be an error to start on bridge before the capacity to add quickly and accurately exists, as there would be too many early disappointments.

Nevertheless, even before a child acquires number skill, there are many attractive trick-taking games which make it fun to play cards and which will develop skills useful for bridge later on. These games which involve play with trumps and without trumps are described in Part 1 and can be started as soon as a child can hold 4 or 5 cards comfortably.

(2) Competence at arithmetic subtraction:
This is not as vital early on as addition but will become important as a child learns playing skills. Counting trumps or the cards missing in a suit (by deducting from 13), counting the high card points missing (by deducting from 40) and similar problems all need to be mastered once the child is already playing bridge.

(3) Physical ability to hold thirteen cards in a fan shape:
Most children have the mental agility to play bridge long before they have the physical capacity to hold thirteen cards in one hand. There are a number of solutions:
(a) Start by playing games which involve holding only 5, 6 or 7 cards.
(b) Allow the child to practice holding 15 cards, 17 cards, 20 cards . . . After a bit of that, 13 cards will seem much easier (child's play!).
(c) Purchase a card-holder. These are not expensive and may consist of a metal tray with two rows to insert the cards or a plastic circular disk in which the cards can be inserted and retained in fan-shape. Of the two, the metal tray is superior and some modern versions have a curved shape to keep the cards concealed from other players.
(d) Use a paper clip and fasten it at the base of the cards. By placing the thumb on the paper clip, it is far easier than normal to produce and retain the fan shape. The paper clip also does rather well on the score of thrift.

THE RIGHT APPROACH
The most important aspects in introducing children to bridge are:
(1) Do not push.
(2) Always use the positive approach. Avoid negative criticism.

(1) Do not push

It does not take parents long to appreciate that children have a natural resistance to doing what parents want them to do. It is a wise parent who avoids the head-to-head confrontations and can direct the child into accepting the parents' wishes by making the child want to do what the parent also wants.

Parents should be aware of what works best. Reverse psychology is one possibility: forbidding or discouraging bridge will make some children want it more. Making bridge an attractive family pastime, an activity in which all can join in, is a sure way to enhance its appeal.

Allowing a child to start bridge as a reward, to make bridge a goal in life ('When you are . . . years old, you will be allowed to learn bridge', 'When you do well at arithmetic, you will be ready for bridge') will work for the achieving child.

If a child resists the prospect of playing bridge, the worst thing you can do is to make an issue of it and try to force the child to learn or to play. The more the parent insists, the more resistant most children become.

Parents who make the mistake of excluding their children from bridge may cause the children to reject bridge throughout their lives. Parents who are engrossed with bridge often turn the child away and the child sees bridge as competing for the parents' affection. Children who are deprived of attention because of bridge will often reject bridge and other cards games later in life.

A common phenomenon is for every second generation to be a card-playing generation. If parents are obsessed with bridge and fall into the trap of being 'too busy', their children may blame bridge for this lack of attention and turn away from it. The same parents when they become grandparents have the time to involve their grandchildren with their games. The grandchildren are delighted to be included and become enthusiastic about playing, even though their own parents scarcely play cards at all.

If a child is exposed to parents quarrelling at the table, it is little wonder that the game is rejected. It is up to the parents to provide the right, friendly atmosphere and include the children in the games. Where the parents display obvious pleasure at the child's participation, you will soon have an enthusiast on your hands. As long as you enjoy these games and do not place stress on the child to perform well, there is no reason why children will not become keen players.

(2) Avoid negative criticism

Parents can extract far greater achievements from children by praising their good efforts than by criticising their errors. The same holds true in the world of bridge. You must remember that there is no reason why beginners should know as much as you do. By praising their successful attempts you will reinforce them. By criticising, you will induce negative feelings towards the activity and instil a sense of insecurity, a loss of self-esteem. There are players who physically tremble when they are playing bridge.

It is just as easy to say, 'That was reasonable but you could have done better', as 'That was a dumb move', but the former is encouraging, while the latter is discouraging. Even if your child takes an obviously silly action (such as raising one heart to two hearts with 15 points), find something positive to say, such as 'You did well to raise my suit, but your hand is a bit too strong for just two hearts.'

Each stage of improvement in your child's progress is worthy of mention and praise. Be genuine and generous with your approval but do not flatter. Children are quick to spot insincerity. Avoid sarcasm at all costs and never, never raise your voice.

Come to think of it, the above all reads as very good advice for the care and handling of partners!

THE BENEFITS AND DANGERS OF BRIDGE FOR CHILDREN

Bridge as a subject taught in schools would have immeasurable benefits. Aside from the mechanical mathematical functions, bridge can develop skill in two areas which are left almost untapped by educational institutions: logical reasoning and partnership co-operation. As most schools do not include bridge in their curricula, parents can do their children a great service by teaching them bridge.

Once a player rises above the elementary stage, skill and success is not primarily a function of mathematical ability. Logical deductions now play a most important role. Within the framework of the game's objectives, logic in bridge resembles the type of logic demonstrated very clearly by Sherlock Holmes to Watson. Almost all card-reading techniques are steeped in Holmesian logic and it is hard to find a superior and more pleasant way of training children in clear thinking.

Children are not naturally adept at co-operating with other children (or with adults!) and there is little in the school setting which will equip them with this social skill. Even team games played at school often amount to no more than a consecutive collection of individual skills. With bridge, by contrast, there is no possibility of regular success in bidding or defence without co-operating with your partner. In learning this, a child will gain a very valuable lesson in life. Of all the aspects of bridge the co-operative factor is the hardest for a child to learn, because it normally does not surface until much later in a child's life.

It would be wrong to suggest there is no danger in learning bridge. Without doubt some promising careers have been cut short through obsession with bridge, but it is the parents' role to identify and redirect any such excessive attention to one particular activity. A multitude of activities can engross a child and obsession with bridge is far less harmful and far more beneficial than many other activities. Far better for your child to spend most spare time with bridge than in front of the TV set or to be bored, have nothing to do, be at a loose end and engage in those harmful activities to which the idle are attracted.

By introducing bridge to your child, you are promoting an activity which will improve your child's memory, concentration and judgment. Bridge is a way of meeting new people and making new friends. It is a game that can be enjoyed for a lifetime, costs very little and can be played regardless of age or physical restrictions.

By teaching bridge to your children, you are providing them with an educational pursuit and a social asset throughout their lives. Even if they do not engage in bridge during their working years, they will still be grateful to you when they decide to retire, for you will have provided them with a stimulating pastime which will keep them mentally fit and mentally alive beyond normal expectations. And if you approach their training in bridge the right way, they will have fond memories of their childhood long after we have all departed from the scene.

PART 1
Card Games For Starters

GAMES TO DEVELOP CARD SENSE PAINLESSLY AS WELL AS
BUILDING A FOUNDATION OF SOUND BRIDGE PRINCIPLES

This part sets out the rules of many games. The age ranges are
suggestions only and if your child can manage games for a higher age
bracket, by all means go ahead and play those games. There are
games for two players, for three players or for four or more players.
All games embody some aspect which will be useful for bridge play
later. Most involve trick-taking and trumps and many have been
adjusted to bridge-like scoring. Familiarity with these games will
make the transition to bridge particularly comfortable.

Chapter 2

Games For Ages 2–5
The Pre-School Child

LEARNING ABOUT THE PACK OF CARDS

Naturally it is vital that your child can recognise all the cards in the pack before you can play the later games. There are many good books that deal with teaching children to read and write even before starting school. Those methods can be applied equally well to teach children the pack of cards.

A blackboard or a whiteboard on which the child can draw freely is very useful. Even painting a wall in the child's room with blackboard paint will do. You can always paint over it when it is no longer needed.

A child of 2 or 3 can quite easily learn to identify all the cards in the pack. Start with just one suit, say diamonds. Take out the ace and the king. Point to the diamond in the middle of the ace and say 'Diamonds'. Cover the As and point to the small diamonds, saying 'Diamonds'. Then point to the A and say 'Ace'. Then combine them with 'Ace of diamonds'. Repeat this procedure with the king, pointing first to the diamond symbol and saying it aloud, followed by the king symbol, and saying that aloud. Then ask your child 'Which one is the ace?' 'Point to the king, darling.'

This is enough for the first session. However, it is worthwhile sticking the ace and the king on to the blackboard so that they are visible throughout the day. Better still if you can put your hands on a dozen or so aces and kings of diamonds, stick them up at the child's eye level all over the house. Blue tac is best as it easily removed without marking the walls or doors. You can play a game of finding the aces and finding the kings, a sort of hide and seek with the cards. You can then allow your child to paste up a few aces and kings for you to find.

If your child has difficulty in recognising the diamonds or distinguishing the ace from the king, leave it and come back to it a few weeks later. If your child quickly distinguishes the ace and king, add the queen next time and repeat the procedure. Once the ace, king and queen are known, add the jack, always staying with just the diamond suit. In addition, spend some time drawing diamonds on the blackboard and colour them red. Allow the child to do the same. If they can try to copy the A, K, Q and J, so much the better, no matter how rough their attempts are.

Having achieved recognition of the top diamonds, do the same with a black suit, say spades. Start with just the ace. Ask the child to find the ace of spades, now the ace of diamonds, now the queen of diamonds, now the ace of spades . . . Then gradually add the king, queen and jack of spades. Again stick up these cards wherever the child usually plays and use the blackboard whenever possible. Do not forget to be effusive with your 'Well done' and 'That's right, darling' whenever the child is correct.

After the top diamonds and spades have been absorbed, add the top hearts and finally the top clubs. Do not start on the number cards until the picture cards have been learnt. If you are confident that the picture cards are well known, you can start on this easy version of *Concentration*. Lay out the 16 picture cards face down in 4 rows of 4. The aim is to locate pairs, two aces or two kings, and so on. The child goes first and turns two cards face up. If they make a pair, the cards are removed and placed face down together beside the child. If they do not match, they are turned face down again in their same positions. It is now your turn and you do the same. A player who matches a pair continues the turn. When a player mismatches, the turn passes to the next player. The player with most pairs wins.

Except where pairs are turned up as a matter of luck, the memory of where the cards are placed helps a player to locate pairs later. When your child is so young, an adult has a huge advantage, of course. Do not be too keen to win and do congratulate the child on each correct pairing that is the result of memory. A fuss and a hug are great rewards for success.

At this stage a shortened version of *Snap* is also possible. Shuffle the 16 cards and deal 8 to child and 8 to you, face down. Each of you takes a card and places it face up simultaneously. If the cards match (two aces or two kings, etc.), call out 'Snap' and place your hand over the cards. The player whose hand is down first wins. Remove the two cards and place them face down in front of the winner. If the cards do not match, play another face up card each. After you have been through the eight cards, players shuffle their remaining cards. Repeat the procedure until all pairs have been matched. Again, at this early stage, do not be too anxious to win. When children are older, they should win only on their merits, but is it important to allow the very young to experience the thrill of winning.

You are ready now to move on to the rest of the pack. Add one card at a time, first the 10 of each suit, then the 9 of each suit, and so on. Do not push ahead unless you are confident your child is competent with the number you have already covered. After every four cards, you can play Concentration and Snap with the extra cards included.

BATTLES

This can be played after the complete pack is known or with a short pack while the cards are still being learnt. Shuffle the pack and deal out the cards. If there is an odd number of players, it does not matter that one or two players have a card more than the others. Each player keeps their pack face down and cards are turned face up, one at a time. These face up cards are called a 'trick'. The highest card face up wins the trick. This is the stage at which the child learns the order of rank of the cards. An ace beats a king, king is higher than a queen, a queen will beat a jack, jack is higher than the 10, a 10 is higher than a 9, and so on. The player who wins the trick takes the cards of the trick and adds them face down to the bottom of their pack. They thus gain more cards in their pack. The game ends when one player wins all the cards or, if the game ends sooner, the winner is the player with most cards.

When two or more players turn up equal high cards, that is when the battles begin. If the tied top cards are 10s or lower, each of the tied players turns up an extra card. The high card wins and the winner takes the trick which consists of all the face up cards. If the tied cards are jacks, again one extra card is played by each tied player. If the tied cards are queens, two cards are played and the highest of the second cards played wins all the cards face up. If the tied cards are kings, three cards are played face up and the highest of the third cards played wins the trick. Where aces are the tied cards, four cards are played face up. The last card played by each player is the one that counts. The highest last card wins the trick, which includes all the played cards.

If there is a tie again when the last card of a battle is played, extra cards are played as above to break the tie.

With this game, children will learn the rank order of the cards and start to associate ace with 4, king with 3 and queen with 2 (which are the values of these cards in bridge terms). In addition, a general impression will be formed that these cards are given more weight than the lower ones.

BATTLES WITH TRUMPS

Once children can cope comfortably with the rank of the cards and play Battles at a reasonable pace, it is an easy step to add the element of trumps to the game. Before dealing out the deals, turn one card face up at random. The suit turned up is the trump suit for that deal. Then deal the cards as for Battles and the play proceeds as for Battles. A trick with no card from the trump suit is won by the highest card on the trick. A trick which includes a trump card is won by the highest trump card. Thus, if diamonds are trumps and one player turns up the ace of spades and the other turns up the 2 of diamonds, the 2 of diamonds will win the trick. Such is the power of trumps.

Where there is a tie of cards, if one of the cards is a trump, there is no battle. The trump card wins. Trumps are not equal. Trumps beat any other suit. If the tied cards do not include a trump, then extra cards are played for Battles, as above.

This method is the speediest way of impressing children with the nature and the power of a trump suit. It is simple, yet effective.

Battles With Trumps can be played with any number of players who can fit comfortably round a table. If you have 6 or more players, it is a good idea to use two packs so that each player has a reasonable number of cards. In this case it is possible to have a tie between two trump cards. If so, extra cards are dealt just as for a regular 'battle'.

FOLLOW SUIT BATTLES
Again a trump suit is chosen and again the cards are divided as equally as possible. The rules for *Battles With Trumps* apply but with this difference:

A trick with a trump card is won by the highest trump card.

A trick with no trump card cannot be won unless there are two cards of the same suit on the trick. If there are not two cards of the same suit, play the next trick. For two players, both cards must be of the same suit and the higher card wins the trick. For 3 players, 2 or 3 cards of the same suit must appear and the highest in that suit wins. The same applies for 4 players but if two cards are of one suit and two of another, nobody wins that trick and the next trick is played.

The winner in all the Battles games is the player who wins most tricks. In this version trump cards are particularly valuable as many tricks will not be won as there are no matching suits. This introduces the child to the concept of 'following suit' in that a trick can be won only if the suits are the same.

If your child can cope with *Battles With Trumps* and *Follow Suit Battles* easily, it is time to move on to the next series of games.

Chapter 3

Games For Ages 5–8
The Early School Years

If your child has reached this age without exposure to cards yet, explain the pack – you will be amazed how quickly a child at these ages will grasp the concept of the suits and the rank of the cards – and play a few games of *Battles*, *Battles With Trumps* and *Follow Suit Battles* in Chapter 2. Provided the pack is known and the concept of trumps is not foreign, you are ready for these games. In all games the bridge pack of 52 cards, no jokers, is used. All play proceeds in clockwise order.

LINGER LONGER

This game can be played by 2 or more players. For 2, 3 or 4 players, deal each player 8 cards face down; for 5 or 6 players, deal 7 cards each. The players pick up their cards and arrange them in suits. The rest of the pack stays face down in the middle of the table, except for the bottom card which is exposed and remains face up to indicate which suit is trumps.

The player on the left of the dealer leads a card face up. Each player in turn (clockwise) must follow suit (play a card of the same suit as the first card). One card from each player makes a trick. The highest card in the suit led will win the trick (except when a trump has been played). If you are unable to follow suit, you may ruff (play a trump card) or you may discard (play a card from another suit, not a trump).

A trick with no trump card is won by the highest card of the suit led.

A trick which includes a trump card is won by the highest trump.

You may lead a trump card if you wish and the others must then play a trump if possible. You must follow suit if you can. When you can follow suit, you may play high or low, as you choose, but there is a significant reward when you win a trick.

The aim is to win tricks. The winner of a trick takes the top card from the face down pack in the middle of the table. The winner thus has an extra card with which to play while all the other players have one card less now. The more tricks you win, the more extra cards you receive and the longer you can stay in the game. Hence the name, *Linger Longer*.

After completion, tricks are removed and placed at the bottom of the face down pile in the middle. As soon as a player runs out of cards, the player drops out of the game. The winner is the last remaining player or if a game stops earlier, the player with most cards when play stops.

FIVE-CARD WHIST

For 2 or more players. Deal 5 cards face down to each player. Players pick up their cards and sort them into suits. The rest of the pack stays face down in the middle of the table, but turn up the top card of the pack for trumps. The player on the left of dealer leads a card face up and each player in turn must follow suit if possible. A trick with a trump card is won by the highest trump; a trick with no trump is won by the highest card of the suit led. The player who wins a trick gathers up the trick and places it face down in front of him. The player who wins a trick leads to the next trick.

Each hand consists of five tricks and you score 10 points for each trick you win. It is convenient to keep a tally and write down each player's score for each hand.

After the hand is over, put the cards played aside and deal a new hand from the rest of the cards (the face down pack in the middle of the table). Replace the card which had indicated trumps and shuffle these cards before the next deal. For 2 players, you can have 5 deals before the complete pack is reshuffled. For 3 players, 3 deals are available and for 4 or 5 players, you can have 2 deals. First player to reach 100 or more is the winner. If there is a tie, play another deal until the tie is broken.

A variation allows play with no trumps. If the top card turned up for trumps is a 2, 3 or 4, play no trumps. If 5 or higher, that suit is trumps.

PARTNERSHIP FIVE-CARD WHIST

For 4 players. Players opposite each other are partners. The play proceeds as in Five-Card Whist. Use the rule where if a 2, 3 or 4 is turned up, the play is no trumps, while if a 5 or higher is turned up, the suit turned up is trumps. At the end of play, partners' tricks are gathered together and the score for each partnership is written down. The first side to 100 wins a game and the winner is the first side to win two games.

Strategy with partnership is a little different. You may be able to win a trick, but it would be foolish to do so if partner has already won the trick. Perhaps you could ruff (play a trump) and win the trick, but if partner is already winning the trick, it may be better to discard and keep your trump for a later trick.

WHIST WITH MORE CARDS

Five-Card Whist is a good game for children that have difficulty in holding many cards in a fan shape. As more and more cards can be held without discomfort, there are several variations which can easily be played.

For 2 players: The rules are the same as for Five-Card Whist but for Deal 1, each player receives 5 cards each, Deal 2 it is 6 cards each, Deal 3 it is 7 cards each and for Deal 4 each player receives 8 cards. For Deals 1, 2 and 3, the trump suit is selected as normal. For Deal 4, there are no cards over, so that play will be at no trumps. Scoring as for Five-Card Whist.

For 3 players: There are 3 deals for each pack, 5 cards each for Deal 1, and 6 each for Deals 2 and 3. On Deal 3 there will be one card left over and that will decide trumps (remember to play no trumps if the card turned up is a 2, 3 or 4). Scoring as above.

For 4 players: There are 2 deals per pack, 6 cards each on Deal 1 and 7 cards each on Deal 2. Play individually or in partnerships (it is more fun in partnerships). There are no cards over for Deal 2, so that play will be at no trumps. Scoring as above. Remember that for Partnership Whist, the side that wins two games first is the winner.

GERMAN WHIST

This is an excellent game for 2 players and the complete version is included in Chapter 4. An abbreviated version which still requires quite some skill is suitable for younger players.

Deal 7 cards to each player. Take turns as dealer. The rest of the pack is placed face down, but the top card is turned up and placed next to the pack. The suit of this card is trumps. Sort your cards into suits and the non-dealer plays a card face up. The dealer plays a card next to it, face up. These two cards make a trick. You must follow suit if you can. A trick with a trump is won by the higher trump. A trick without a trump is won by the higher card in the suit led. If second player did not follow suit and did not ruff (play a trump), first player wins the trick.

The player who wins the trick gathers the trick and places it face down beside him. The winner of the trick then picks up the exposed card next to the pack and adds it to his hand. The trick loser takes the top card from the pack and, without showing it to the other player, adds it to his hand. The next card from the pack is now turned face up and placed next to the pack.

The player who wins a trick leads to the next trick. After each trick the winner adds the exposed card to his hand, the loser adds the top card from the pack to his hand and the next card in the pack is then exposed. When all the cards from the pack have been used, play continues until each player has played all his cards.

Each deal consists of 26 tricks. The player who wins more tricks is the winner. You score 10 points for each trick you have more than your opponent. If it was 13 tricks apiece, there is no score. If you won 14-12, you score 20. A win by 15-11 scores 40, a win by 16-10 scores 60, and so on. A game is first to 100 and the winner is the first player to win two games.

There are two key elements of strategy in this game. Because the winner of the trick receives the exposed card, you would try to win the trick if the exposed card is particularly valuable (such as a known winner, a trump or a very high card in a suit even though not a winner). If the exposed card is useless, you would not mind giving away a trick in the hope of picking up a better card from the top of the pack. Still, it is an advantage to have the lead. Then if the next exposed card is very valuable and it is your lead, you may be able to play a sure winner to make sure you can add the exposed card to your hand.

The other element is memory. It is a great advantage to be able to remember which cards have gone, how many trumps are left and which cards in which each suit are now high. This comes with practice and can be left until the complete game is explained in Chapter 4.

OH HELL!

Oh Hell! is a fun game for young and old. It is an excellent family game and can be perfectly enjoyed by adults only. It is best with 3 or more players. A more advanced version will appear in Chapter 4.

The game consists of 13 deals. On the first deal, each player receives 1 card, on the second deal 2 cards and so on to the 7th deal where it is 7 cards each. On the 8th deal, it is back to 6 cards, then 5 cards each and so on until it is 1 card each for the 13th deal. If there are 8 players, there would be only 11 deals, from 1 card each to 6 cards each and back again. Similarly, for 9 or 10 players (the more, the merrier), there would be just 9 deals, from 1 card each to 5 cards each and back again.

Cut for dealer. Highest card is the dealer. Shuffle and deal the cards, clockwise order as normal.

After the cards have been dealt, the rest of the pack is put aside and not used during the play. The top card of the remainder is turned face up and this suit is trumps during the deal. The player on the left of the dealer now 'bids'. He states how many tricks he thinks he will win. The minimum is, of course, zero and the maximum is the number of cards in hand. It is a good idea to give each player half a dozen matches. When bidding the player can then put the number of matches in front of him to indicate the number of tricks he intends to win. Thus, if you think you can win 2 tricks, put 2 matches in front of you, etc. This saves arguments later about the actual number of tricks stated.

Each player in turn clockwise bids for a specific number of tricks. The last player to bid is the dealer. After the bidding is over, the player on the left of dealer leads a card. Each player in turn must follow suit if he can. If unable to follow suit, he may ruff (play a trump) or discard (play a card other than a trump). After each player has played to the trick, the winner gathers up the trick. A trick without a trump is won by the card of the suit led. A trick with a trump is won by the highest trump. The winner places the trick face down in front of him and then leads to the next trick. Play continues until all tricks have been played.

The number of tricks for which you have bid is called your 'contract'. Your object is to win that number of tricks, not more and not less. If you succeed, you have made your contract. If you fail, you have 'burst'. If you bid for 0 tricks, you will try to win no tricks. If you have bid for 2 tricks, you will make your contract if you win exactly 2 tricks. If you win 1 or 3 or more, you have 'burst'.

When play ends, players check whether they made their contract or whether they have burst. The score for each player is recorded. If you burst, you lose 2 points for each trick by which you missed your contract. If you missed by two tricks, you score –4. If you made your contract, you receive +10 plus 2 points for each trick you won. If you made a contract of 3 tricks, you would score +16. The winner is the player with the most points after all the deals have been played.

There is considerable skill in estimating the number of tricks you can win and playing to win that number. Your bid may be influenced by the number of tricks bid by players ahead of you. The more bids ahead of you, the better you can gauge the strength of the other players' hands. There is skill in the play not only in winning tricks but also in getting rid of unwanted high cards when you need no more tricks. Oh, the name 'Oh Hell' refers to the only acceptable exclamation that can be made when you 'burst'. Games often explode with great hilarity.

Oh Hell! is excellent not only in dealing with trumps and tricks, but also in introducing the concepts of bidding and contract and the winning of a specific number of tricks. The author used to start bridge classes for absolute beginners by playing *Oh Hell!*. The students had fun and quickly learnt about tricks, trumps, bidding and contract. One major difference is that in bridge you are allowed to win more tricks than your contract while in *Oh Hell!* you must win the exact number.

Chapter 4

Games For Ages 8 Up
Ready For Anything

At this stage, it is assumed your child is familiar with the pack of cards and concepts such as tricks and trumps.

TEA FOR TWO – for 2 players only
Use a short pack consisting only of the A, K, Q, J and 10 of each suit. Shuffle and deal 10 cards to each player. Turn up a card at random from the rest of the pack to determine the trump suit. If a 2 or 3 is turned up, play no trumps. If a 4 or higher is turned up, the suit of that card becomes trumps.

The non-dealer plays a card face-up and the dealer does the same. These two cards form a trick and the higher card wins the trick. The aim is to win 6 tricks or more. You must follow suit, if possible. If unable to follow suit, you may ruff (play a trump) or discard (play another suit, not a trump). A trick with a trump is won by the higher trump. A trick without a trump is won by the higher card in the suit led.

Scoring: You score 10 points for each trick you win above 5. Only one player can therefore score points on each deal. If you win all ten tricks, you score a bonus of 50 points. First to score 100 points wins a game. First to win two games is the overall winner.

For strong players, this game is trivial since the other player's cards are known. However, for children and newcomers to trick-taking games, the game includes important concepts such as counting the cards and planning endplays. For example, if you hold A-Q-J-10 in a suit, you know that when you play the ace, the king must fall. There are only 5 cards in each suit. Likewise, if you have A-K-10, you know that the queen and jack will fall when you play the ace and king, and your 10 will then be a winner. By keeping track of the cards played by your opponent, you can work out how to score the maximum tricks.

For example, suppose spades became trumps and you hold:

♠ A K Q J — It is your lead and you have 8 obvious winners,
♡ Q — the 4 trumps, the A-K-Q of diamonds and the ace
♢ A K Q — of clubs. However, you can make sure of 9 tricks by
♣ A Q — playing off your spade and diamond winners and
keeping track of what your opponent discards. You start with the
spades (it is a good idea to draw trumps when you have more than
your opposition) and then the diamonds. Your opponent will have
three cards left. If he has thrown 2 clubs, then the king of clubs will
now be singleton and you play the ace and queen of clubs. If only one
club has been thrown, your opponent will have K-x left in clubs and
the ace of hearts. Play the queen of hearts and force your opponent to
lead clubs to you, thus guaranteeing you two club tricks. This type of
thinking is invaluable later in bridge play.

OH HELL! – for 2 or more players

This was described in Chapter 3, pages 23 and 24. Please refer to
those pages for the method of play and the scoring. Once you have
played that version for some time, it is time to add this rule which
makes the game a bit tougher:

The dealer (who is last to bid) must make a bid so that the total
number of tricks bid does not equal the number of tricks available.

For example, suppose each player has 5 cards so that 5 tricks are
available. When the bidding reaches the dealer, the previous bids
have been for 1, 1 and 2 tricks, a total of 4. The dealer is obliged to bid
for 0 tricks or 2 or more tricks. A bid for 1 trick would make the game
'friendly' and each player could theoretically make the contract. By
requiring the dealer to make it 'unfriendly', at least one player is
bound to fail to win the required tricks.

With this rule in use, there is a significant disadvantage in being the
dealer, especially when dealing just 1 or 2 cards per player. You can
imagine a situation with 1 card each where a player has already bid
for 1 trick and the dealer, not permitted to bid for no tricks, must say
1 trick on the most worthless of cards. *Oh Hell!*

OH HELL! – for 4 players

In the basic version of *Oh Hell!*, there are 13 rounds, starting with 1 card each up to 7 cards each and back down to 1 card each. Where there are four players, the game can be improved by going from 1 card each up to 13 cards each. On the round where there are 13 cards each, the play is no trumps. On other rounds, the top card of the remainder of the pack is turned up to indicate the trump suit: if a 2, 3 or 4 is turned up, play no trumps; if a 5 or higher is turned up, the suit becomes the trump suit for that deal.

It is worthwhile to give children practice with no trumps. One advantage of going up to 13 cards is that the estimate of the tricks can be much more accurate when most of the cards have been dealt. When you are up to 10, 11 or 12 cards each, there are not as many nasty shocks of having an ace or a king ruffed on the first round of a suit. If you wish, you may go from 1 card to 13 and back to 1 again. The scoring is the same for standard *Oh Hell!* (see page 24).

TRIO – for 3 players

Use a normal pack and cut for dealer. Players become dealer in turn. Each player is dealt 16 cards, the remaining four (the 'widow') stay face down for the moment. The dealer studies his cards and then declares the trump suit (or no trumps). He then picks up the cards in the widow and discards any four cards face down, so that he is left with 16 cards. The player on the left of the dealer then leads a card, 2nd player follows suit if possible and the dealer follows suit if possible. Those 3 cards form a trick and the winner of the trick gathers it in, places it face down in front of him and leads to the next trick. Normal rules apply: a trick with a trump is won by the highest trump, a trick with no trump is won by the highest card of the suit led. If unable to follow suit, you may ruff or discard.

There are 16 tricks and each player is required to win a specific number of tricks: *Dealer:* 8 tricks, *dealer's left:* 5 tricks, *dealer's right:* 3 tricks. These numbers for each player are the 'contracts'. The object is to make your contract or more.

SCORING:

If you make your contract, you score zero. For each trick more than your contract, you receive plus points:

No trumps; or spades or hearts as trumps: 30 points for each overtrick. *Clubs or diamonds as trumps:* 20 points for each overtrick.

If you fail to make your contract, you receive minus points, –50 for each undertrick (each trick by which you missed). For example, if the dealer makes only 6 tricks, he scores –100. Game is first to +100 and first player to win 2 games is the overall winner.

Variations: It may be difficult for children to hold 16 cards. If so, play with a short pack and the trick requirements then are as follows:

Cards to be used		Tricks to be won by each player		
	Cards & widow	Dealer	Left of dealer	Right of dealer
A, K, Q, J and 10	6 each widow 2	3 tricks	2 tricks	1 trick
A, K, Q, J, 10 and 9	7 each widow 3	3 tricks	2 tricks	2 tricks
A, K, Q, J, 10, 9 and 8	8 each widow 4	4 tricks	2 tricks	2 tricks
A, K, Q, J, 10, 9, 8, 7	9 each widow 5	4 tricks	3 tricks	2 tricks
A, K, Q, J, 10, 9, 8, 7, 6	10 each widow 2	5 tricks	3 tricks	2 tricks
A, K, Q, J, 10, 9, 8, 7, 6, 5	11 each widow 3	6 tricks	3 tricks	2 tricks
From ace to 4 inclusive	14 each widow 2	7 tricks	4 tricks	3 tricks

The dealer clearly has two great advantages, the ability to declare the trump suit and the exchange of cards with the widow. That is why the dealer's contract is significantly higher than the others.

Another variation to *Trio* applies only after the first deal has been completed. Any player who has won 1 or more overtricks can improve his hand as follows: he is allowed to pass poor cards from his own hand to one or both opponents and receive better cards in return. The total number passed is equal to the number of overtricks won on the preceding deal. Suppose the dealer made 3 overtricks. On the next deal, he may pass 3 cards to 1 player or 2 to one and 1 to the other. Those players must give back a higher card in the same suit as the suit passed. If unable to do so, they return the card passed. If two players scored overtricks, the one who won more tricks in total goes first. The passing of cards takes place before the trump suit is declared and before the dealer has picked up the widow. This variation makes the game a lot of fun but we would not go as far as some do who require that players must give back the *highest* card in the suit passed to them. This is too great an advantage.

This is the first game where the trump suit is not a matter of random luck. Here the dealer stipulates the trump suit or no trumps.

GERMAN WHIST – for 2 players only

An abbreviated version of this excellent game appeared in Chapter 3, page 22. In the full version, each player receives 13 cards. The rest of the pack is face down but the top card is turned face up beside the pack. This card determines the trump suit: if a 2, 3 or 4 is turned up, play no trumps, otherwise trumps is the suit of the card turned up. The non-dealer leads a card and the dealer must follow suit if possible. These two cards form a trick. The winner of the trick adds the face up card beside the pack to his hand, the loser takes the top face down card from the top of the pack. Each player thus has 13 cards again. The next card from the top of the pack is now turned face up before the next trick is played. The winner of a trick gathers up the cards in the trick, placing them face down beside him, and leads to the next trick.

Tricks with a trump card are won by the higher trump. Tricks with no trump are won by the higher card in the suit led. There are 26 tricks in all. After 13 tricks, the face down pack is exhausted but play continues until all cards have been played. After the pack has been exhausted, *you are obliged to ruff if unable to follow suit.*

The rule requiring you to ruff if you cannot follow suit applies only after there are no more cards to be added to your hand. While there are still cards to be picked up from the pack, you may ruff or discard when unable to follow suit.

If you are unable to follow suit, you must announce this to the other player whenever you pick up a card of this suit from the pack. It applies whether you ruffed or discarded when you showed out. For example, suppose your opponent leads a spade and you have none. You lose this trick, say, but pick up a spade from the pack. You must now say, 'I have a spade.' Each time you pick up another spade from the pack, you must announce, 'I have another spade.'

SCORING
There is no score if each player wins 13 tricks. For each trick over 13, the winner scores as follows:
Spades or hearts are trumps: 30 points for each trick above 13.
Diamonds or clubs are trumps: 20 points for each trick above 13.
No trumps: 40 points for trick 14, 30 points for each additional trick.

Game is first to 100 and the winner is the first player to win 2 games. Bonus points are awarded: 700 points for a win by 2 games to nil, 500 points for a win by 2 games to 1. In addition, if a game is won by 19 tricks to 7, or by a greater margin, the winner scores 500 ('small slam') bonus for that game. If a game is won by 22 tricks to 4 or a greater margin, the winner scores a 1000 ('grand slam') bonus for that game.

German Whist is great for mental training. A key element for success is keeping track of the cards as they go and knowing which cards are high in each suit. Bridge players can improve their card memory by regular games of *German Whist* with another competent player.

The face up card determines whether you should try to win the trick or whether you are likely to do better with a face down card from the pack. Having the lead is an advantage. If a high card turns face up, you are in a position to benefit by leading a sure winner and thus adding a valuable card to your hand as well as winning a trick. It will often pay you to build up length in one suit (other than just the trump suit). Later you can play your winners in this suit and force your opponent to use up his trumps.

SOLO – for 4 players

Two standard packs are used but only one pack is used at a time. While one pack is being dealt, the other is shuffled ready for the next deal. This saves waiting. Each player is dealt 13 cards. The top card of the other pack is turned face up to select trumps. The player on the left of the dealer bids first and each player bids in turn, clockwise. If you do not wish to make a bid, say 'Pass'. A player who has passed may not bid later (except for Prop and Cop, see later). If all players pass on the first round, there is no play and the next dealer deals a fresh hand.

After a bid has been made, the next player must make a higher bid or pass. The order of bids is as follows:

Proposal and Acceptance (popularly known as 'prop' and 'cop'): One player calls 'prop' which is an offer to take any of the other players as partner and attempt to win 8 or more tricks. A hand which is worth about 4 tricks is suitable for a prop. Any subsequent player may say 'cop' and agree to partner the 'prop' player. A player who has already passed may still 'cop'. This is the only variation where players are partners against the other two. Unlike whist or bridge, partners may be next to each other or opposite each other. If a player props and no one accepts, the prop player may amend his call to a higher bid. If not, the hand is thrown in and the next dealer deals a new hand.

Solo: This ranks above Prop and Cop. A player who bids 'solo' undertakes to win 5 or more tricks with the turned up suit as trumps.

Abundance Out: This ranks above solo and undertakes to win 9 tricks with a trump suit other than the one turned up. A player simply calls 'abundance out' and does not declare the trump suit unless his is the highest bid and the other three players have passed. He then declares the trump suit before the first card is led.

Abundance In: This ranks above abundance out and is an undertaking to win 9 tricks with the turned up suit as trumps.

Abundance Declared: This is the highest call of all and undertakes to win all 13 tricks with no trumps. The player who makes this call leads to the first trick. In all other cases, the first lead is made by the player on dealer's left.

The bids of *Misere* and *Open Misere* have been deliberately omitted as these provide no value in learning bridge. *Misere* is an undertaking to take no tricks and ranks just above *Solo*. *Open Misere* is the same as *Misere* (an undertaking to win no tricks) but after the first trick is over, the caller places his remaining 12 cards face up and plays them exposed. *Open Misere* ranks above *Abundance In* in the calling.

After the bidding, the player on the left of dealer leads a card and each player in clockwise order follows suit if possible. The four face up cards form a trick. As usual, a trick with a trump is won by the highest trump and a trick with no trump is won by the highest card of the suit led. The player who wins a trick gathers it in, placing it face down beside him, and leads to the next trick. After the 13 tricks have been played, the players check to see whether the call made has succeeded.

SCORING:

For prop and cop: If successful, the winners receive 4 units plus 1 unit for each trick above 8. If prop and cop fails, the opponents score 4 points plus 1 point for each trick over 6 won by them.

For solo: 4 points from each player to the caller if *Solo* succeeded; 4 points to each player by the caller if unsuccessful. In addition, 1 extra point is scored for each overtrick or extra undertrick. Thus, if the caller wins only 3 tricks, he loses 15 and each opponent wins 5.

For abundance out or abundance in: 12 points from each player to the caller if successful; 12 points to each player by the caller if not successful. For each overtrick or extra undertrick, 2 points from or to each opponent.

For abundance declared: 24 points from or to each opponent. (*Misere* is 8 points from or to each opponent and *Open Misere* is 16.) There are no overtricks or undertricks in abundance declared, misere or open misere. Play ends as soon as the contract fails or after trick 13 if it is successful.

Solo is a challenging game in itself. It is useful en route to bridge as it features estimating how many tricks you can win, bidding by all four players and occasionally partnership play.

Chapter 5

From Whist To Bridge
For Ages 8 & Over

Whist was the forerunner of most trick-taking games including Solo and Bridge. Whist tournaments existed during the 19th century and the first recorded bridge games in England and the United States occurred in the early 1890s. The following variations of whist offer a gentle progression into the world of bridge.

The rules about shuffling, dealing and trick-taking are common to all the games that follow. Unless stated otherwise, there are 4 players in two partnerships. Partners sit opposite each other. Before play starts, players draw cards for partners, the two highest against the two lowest. Two packs of cards are used, but only one is in play. While the cards are dealt, the dealer's partner shuffles the other pack and places it on the right, ready for the next dealer. The dealer passes the shuffled pack to the player on his right to 'cut' (take some cards from the top of the pack and place them face down beside the pack). The dealer completes the cut, taking the rest of the pack and placing it on top of the cut cards. The cards are then dealt, one at a time, starting on the left, until all the cards are dealt. There are 52 cards and each player receives 13.

It is customary not to pick up any cards until the deal is completed. Then, if a misdeal has occurred (one player has 14 cards, another has only 12), it can be corrected if the cards have not been seen. If players have looked at their cards and a misdeal occurs, the pack is reshuffled and the same dealer redeals the hand.

In the play, you must follow suit if possible. A 'revoke' or a 'renege' is failure to follow suit when you could. If a revoke is established, the offender has to give two tricks to the opponents. If unable to follow suit, you may ruff (play a trump) or discard (play a card from another suit, not a trump). A trick with a trump is won by the highest trump. A trick without a trump is won by the highest card in the suit led.

Unless advised otherwise, the player on the left of the dealer starts the play by playing a card face up (i.e. he leads to the first trick or 'makes the opening lead'). Each player in turn (clockwise) then plays a card. The 4 cards faced up form a trick. In each game there are 13 tricks. The player who wins a trick gathers up the cards and places them face down beside him. One member of a partnership generally collects all the tricks for the partnership. The player who wins a trick leads to the next trick. In writing about bridge it is convenient to call the four players North (N), South (S), East (E) and West (W), with N-S being one partnership playing against E-W, the other partnership.

This is purely a labelling device and there is no requirement that players must sit at the compass positions at the table.

Scoring: The first 6 tricks won by a partnership are called the 'book' and score no points. Scores for the 7th and subsequent tricks are:

No trumps: 40 for the 7th trick, 30 for each additional trick.

Spades or hearts as trumps: 30 for each trick over 6.

Diamonds or clubs as trumps: 20 for each trick over 6.

Game is first to 100. When a game ends, each side starts from zero again. A rubber is best of 3 games. A rubber ends when one side wins two games. Bonus points are awarded when a side wins its second game: +700 if the game score then is 2-0, +500 if the score is 2-1.

GAME 1 – NO TRUMPS WHIST

13 cards each. No bidding. No trump suit. Player on the left of the dealer leads to the first trick. After 13 tricks have been played, enter the score for the winning side. There is no score for the losers.

An important difference when playing in partnership is to note the card played by partner. You may be able to win a trick but it could be foolish to do so if partner's card is already winning. If you are 3rd or 4th player, always check partner's card before playing.

STRATEGY AT NO TRUMPS:

Prefer to lead your longest suit and keep on with that suit. When the others run out, your remaining cards in that suit will be winners, since they cannot win the trick if they cannot follow suit and there is no trump suit. As players lead their own long suit, it is best to return partner's led suit when you win a trick, unless you have a strong suit of your own. One usually avoids returning a suit led by the opposition.

The card to lead: When playing for yourself, it hardly matters which card you lead in any suit. As whist and bridge are partnership games, you can help your partner by following certain rules about which cards to lead.

Lead top card from a sequence of three or more cards headed by the ten or higher (e.g. from K-Q-J-5, lead the K; from J-10-9-8, lead the J). The top five cards in each suit – A, K, Q, J, 10 – are called the 'honour cards' or 'honours'. Lead top of a sequence only when the sequence includes at least one honour.

Lead fourth-highest (fourth from the top) where the long suit has no such three-card or longer sequence (e.g. from K-J-8-4-3, lead the 4).

Play by 2nd player to a trick: Unless you have a lot of high cards in the suit led, play low in second position and give partner a chance to win the trick. If you know partner cannot win the trick (e.g. an opponent leads the king and you have the ace), it is sensible for you to win the trick. You may also know from the previous play that partner has no useful high cards in the suit led. Again, you may then depart from the general principle, second-hand-low, and try to win the trick yourself.

Play by 3rd player to a trick: Partner has already played to this trick. Try to win the trick by playing your highest card ('third-hand-high'), unless partner's card is good enough to win anyway. If you have equally high cards, win the trick or try to win with the cheapest card possible.

Play by 4th player to a trick: If partner's card is winning the trick, play low (unless you need to take the lead). If an opponent is winning the trick, beat their card with the cheapest card possible. If unable to beat their card, play your lowest card in the suit.

If unable to follow suit, discard your most worthless card.

GAME 2 – TRUMPS WHIST

13 cards each. The top card of the other pack is turned up as the trump suit. This card is left face-up during the play to remind each of the players which suit is trumps. There is still no bidding.

A trick with no trump card is won by the highest card of the suit led, but a trick with a trump card is won by the highest trump.

Throughout the play, you are still obliged to follow suit, of course. If you are unable to follow suit at trumps, you are permitted to ruff. However, you are not obliged to do so and you may choose to discard a worthless card instead of ruffing. As you are not forced to ruff when out of a suit, you will decide whether to ruff or whether to discard. It is sensible to ruff a winning card played by an opponent but it might be unwise to ruff if partner's card will win the trick anyway. Remember, you are partners. If you are in second position and could ruff, you should prefer to discard if there is some chance that partner could win the trick. Play second-hand-low and keep your trump for another trick later. However, if you know partner cannot win the trick, by all means ruff.

Scoring is the same as on page 34.

GAME 3 – TRUMPS AND NO TRUMPS

13 cards each. The top card of the other pack is turned face up. If a 2, 3 or 4 is turned up, the game is to be played with no trumps. If a higher card is turned up, the suit of the face-up card is trumps. This card is left face-up to remind players of the trump suit or no trumps. The play and scoring is the same as Games 1 and 2. Game 3 is simply a combined version of Games 1 and 2.

GAME 4 – DEALER'S WHIST

13 cards each. The dealer, after examining his cards and without consulting partner, declares the trump suit or no trumps. This gives the dealer some control over the selection of trumps, whereas in Games 2 and 3, the card turned up as trumps (or no trumps) is purely a matter of luck. When dealer, choose only a suit with five or more cards as your trump suit. With no five-card or longer suit, usually prefer to choose no-trumps. Play and scoring as before.

GAME 5 - PARTNERSHIP WHIST

This is the same as Game 4 except that the dealer and the dealer's partner discuss whether to play in trumps or no trumps. This gives the dealer's side a much better chance of discovering a good trump suit.

The dealer and dealer's partner make one suggestion ('bid') at a time, nominating a trump suit or no trumps. The dealer makes the first bid. If partner agrees, that decides the trump suit or no trumps. If partner disagrees, partner makes an alternative suggestion. If no trump suit is agreed after three turns each, the hand is to be played with no trumps. Play and scoring as before.

GAME 6 - DECLARER'S WHIST

The most valuable cards are the high cards in each suit, the ace, king, queen and jack. These are more likely to win tricks than the lower cards. We estimate the value of our hand by alloting points for these cards. They are called high card points (HCP).

$$A = 4 \qquad K = 3 \qquad Q = 2 \qquad J = 1$$

Each player counts the high card points in his hand. Starting with the dealer, each player calls out the total number of points held. The player who has most points becomes the 'declarer'. If there is a tie for the most points held, the declarer will be the dealer (if involved in the tie) or the player nearest the dealer (if the dealer is not involved in the tie . . . nearest goes according to clockwise direction).

The rest of the game is the same as Game 4, except that the declarer (rather than the dealer) declares what is to be trumps or whether play is to be at no trumps or not.

GAME 7 - DUMMY WHIST WITHOUT POINTS

13 cards each. *The partner of the dealer puts his 13 cards face up neatly in suits on the table.* These exposed cards are called the 'dummy'. The declarer is the partner of the dummy and declares the trump suit or no trumps.

To choose a trump suit, the suit should have 8 or more cards in the combined hands. If more than one trump suit is available, choose a major suit (spades or hearts) rather than a minor suit (diamonds or clubs), as the majors score more. If the suits are both majors or both minors, choose the longer, or if both have the same length, choose the stronger. If there is no suit which has 8 or more trumps together, usually prefer to play no trumps. Being able to see partner's hand gives the dealer's side an even better chance of finding no trumps or the best suit for trumps.

After trumps or no trumps has been declared, the player on declarer's left makes the first lead. Play proceeds as before but *declarer must play both hands, his own and the dummy*. The dummy player takes no part in the play. If dummy wins a trick, the next lead comes from dummy, while if declarer wins, the next lead must come from declarer's hand.

Scoring: Same as usual if declarer wins seven or more tricks. However, if declarer fails to win seven tricks or more, the other side will score bonus points at the rate of 50 for each trick by which declarer failed. For example, if declarer made only four tricks, the other side would score 150 bonus points, since declarer failed by three tricks. Bonus points do not count towards scoring a game. Only the declarer side can score points towards game. Bonus points are still valuable since they count in your total points at the end of the rubber.

GAME 8 – DUMMY WHIST
Each player counts the high card points (HCP), using A = 4, K = 3, Q = 2 and J = 1. Starting with the dealer, each player calls out the total number of HCP held. The side which has more points becomes the declarer side and the partner that has more points becomes the declarer. Dummy is revealed and declarer nominates the trump suit or no trumps. (The pack has 40 HCP. If each side has 20, redeal the hand. For a tie within the declarer side, the one nearer the dealer will be the declarer.)

The play proceeds as before. *The player left of declarer makes the opening lead.* Declarer plays both dummy and his own hand.

Scoring: If declarer scores seven tricks or more, scoring is as usual. If declarer fails to win seven tricks, the opponents score bonus points. *Only the declarer side can score points for game.* Where the declarer side has not won a game ('not vulnerable'), the opponents score 50 bonus points for each trick by which they have defeated declarer. The rate is 50 points per undertrick regardless of which suit is trumps or whether no trumps is played. Where the declarer side has won a game ('vulnerable'), the opponents will score 100 points for each trick by which they have defeated declarer. 'Vulnerable' and 'Not vulnerable' are just bridge jargon, referring to the status in the rubber of 'having won one game' and 'not having won a game'.

DUMMY WHIST FOR 3 PLAYERS

Deal 13 cards to each player and 13 cards face down as a 'widow'. Count your HCP. Starting with the dealer, each player calls out his total HCP. The player with the highest total becomes the declarer. In the case of a tie, the player nearest to the dealer becomes declarer.

By deducting the HCP total for the 3 players from 40, the number of HCP in the widow hand will be known. The hand with the second highest HCP total becomes the dummy and is placed opposite declarer. If it is the widow, this hand is revealed as the dummy. If a player holds the second strongest hand, this becomes the dummy and that player picks up and plays the widow hand. (In the case of a tie, the widow hand becomes dummy or declarer selects which hand is to be dummy.)

The game now proceeds as for Dummy Whist. The trump suit is declared, the player on declarer's left makes the opening lead, declarer has to play dummy's cards as well as his own, and so on. The rate of scoring is the same, but separate scores have to be kept for each player, as there will be different partnerships from time to time.

As the declarer side has more points than the defenders, the declarer side is more likely to succeed in taking seven or more tricks. This is not certain, of course, as there is skill both in declarer play and defence.

The existence of the dummy separates Bridge from other trick-taking games. From the first lead, each player sees half the pack (13 cards in hand + cards in dummy). This single factor transforms Bridge into essentially a game of skill. Other games suffer a significant defect because of the large luck factor involved. Because the dummy cards are revealed, it is possible to plan your play as declarer or as a defender with great accuracy. In fact, hundreds of books have been written about the play of the cards at bridge.

GAME 9 – BIDDING WHIST

Starting with the dealer, each player states the number of HCP held. The side with more points is the declarer side and the two partners discuss which suit shall be trumps or whether to play no trumps. Each partner in turn makes a bid. A bid is simply a suggestion to partner of a trump suit or no trumps. The bidding (also known as the 'auction') continues until agreement is reached.

A suggested trump suit must contain at least four cards. With no particularly long suit and no void ('void' = no cards in a suit) and no singleton (one card in a suit), it is usually best to suggest no trumps at once. If there is no early agreement and neither partner insists on a suit, one of the partners should suggest no trumps. After agreement, the first player to suggest the agreed trump suit or no trumps is declarer.

In the play, the player on the left of the declarer makes the opening lead *before seeing dummy*. After the lead, dummy's 13 cards are placed face up (in suits), facing declarer. Trumps go on dummy's right. The scoring is the same as for Game 8.

GAME 10 – CONTRACT WHIST

The early play proceeds exactly as Game 9 – see above. However, instead of needing to win just seven or more tricks, the declarer is required to win a specific number of tricks depending on the total points held by declarer and dummy:

20-22 points: 7 or more tricks in no trumps
                8 or more tricks with a trump suit
23-25 points: 8 or more tricks in no trumps
                9 or more tricks with a trump suit
26-32 points: 9 or more tricks in no trumps
                10 more more tricks with ♡ or ♠ as trumps
                11 or more tricks with ♣ or ♢ as trumps
33-36 points: 12 or more tricks
37-40 points: All 13 tricks

Play: The opening lead is made before dummy appears.

Scoring: The same as for Game 9, but to score points declarer must win the number of tricks stipulated or more. If not, the defenders score bonus points of 50 (if the declarer side is not vulnerable) or 100 (if the declarer is vulnerable) for each trick by which declarer fails.

If declarer is required to win 12 tricks ('small slam') and does so, the declarer side scores an extra bonus of 500 when not vulnerable or 750 vulnerable. If declarer is required to win all 13 tricks ('grand slam') and does so, the declarer side scores an extra 1000 not vulnerable or 1500 vulnerable.

CONTRACT WHIST FOR 3 PLAYERS

Deal 13 cards each and 13 face down as a widow hand. Players call out their HCP. The players with most HCP is the declarer. The hand with the second highest HCP total becomes the dummy. If it is the widow hand, that is revealed as dummy. If it is a player's hand, it is also revealed as the dummy and that player picks up the widow hand and plays those cards as his own from there on.

After dummy is revealed, declarer nominates the trump suit (or no trumps) and the player on declarer's left makes the opening lead. The total of declarer's HCP + dummy's HCP is known and the number of tricks declarer must win is based on the scale for the total HCP held (see opposite page). Play continues as normal and after all tricks have been played, the score is recorded as above, depending on whether declarer made his contract or failed. A separate scoresheet needs to be kept for each player, as there will be different partnerships from time to time.

Dummy Whist For 3 and *Contract Whist For 3* are both good games to play, even for bridge players, when you are unable to arrange a foursome.

Rubber Bridge Scoring Table

CONTRACT POINTS

Contract points count towards game and are written under the line.
Only the declarer side can score contract points.

No-trumps – First trick 40
                   Subsequent tricks 30
Spades or Hearts (major suits) 30
Diamonds or Clubs (minor suits) 20
Final contract doubled and made: Double above values
Final contract redoubled and made: Above values x 4

DECLARER BONUS POINTS

OVERTRICKS		*Not vulnerable*	*Vulnerable*
For each	Not doubled..................	Trick value	Trick value
overtrick	Doubled..........................	100	200
	Redoubled......................	200	400
SLAMS BID AND MADE:		*Not vulnerable*	*Vulnerable*
Small slam......................................		500	750
Grand slam		1000	1500

FOR MAKING A DOUBLED OR REDOUBLED
CONTRACT: 50

FOR COMPLETING A RUBBER:

For winning by two games to nil 700
For winning by two games to one 500
For one game if rubber is unfinished 300
For partscore if rubber is unfinished 50

FOR HONOURS:

Four trump honours in one hand 100
Five trump honours in one hand 150
Four aces in one hand if contract is NT 150
(Honours are claimed at the conclusion of the hand.)

DEFENDERS' BONUS POINTS
FOR DEFEATING A CONTRACT:

Not doubled, each undertrick is 50 not vulnerable, 100 vulnerable
Doubled but not vulnerable, 1st undertrick 100, others 200
Doubled and vulnerable, 1st undertrick 200, others 300
Redoubled: All undertricks score at twice the doubled rate

FOR HONOURS

Same as for the declarer side.

PART 2

Acol Bridge
For Children

A SIMPLIFIED APPROACH TO BIDDING

This part includes the rules of Bridge, an outline of basic scoring, simplified bidding according to the Acol system, basic leads and signals, tips on declarer play and defence, and illustrations of what has been achieved by young masters around the world.

Chapter 6

The Rules Of Bridge

If you already know the rules of bridge, skip over to the next chapter. If you have been playing the games in Chapter 5, you will be familiar with the basic concepts (tricks, trumps, following suit, declarer, dummy, and so on) and should move on to page 47, starting with The Bidding. Otherwise, if you are starting here, this outline should dispel any doubts you might have about the rules or procedure when playing bridge.

HOW THE GAME IS PLAYED

Bridge is a game for four players, playing in two partnerships. It is a head-to-head battle – your side against their side. Partners sit opposite each other. Partnerships are chosen by agreement or by lot. The most common method is for each player to choose a card from the pack fanned out face down, with the players selecting the two highest cards as one partnership against the players selecting the two lowest cards.

THE BRIDGE PACK

A standard pack of 52 cards is used. There are no jokers and no cards of any exceptional rank or function (unlike 500 where jacks have a special role, or Canasta where 2s are jokers).

There are four suits:

♠ SPADES – ♡ HEARTS – ◇ DIAMONDS – ♣ CLUBS

Each suit has 13 cards in order: A, K, Q, J, 10, 9, 8, 7, 6, 5, 4, 3, 2. An ace beats a king, a king beats a queen, a queen beats a jack, a jack beats a ten and so on. The top five cards in each suit, the A, K, Q, J and 10, are known as the honour cards or honours.

The suits also have a ranking order: CLUBS (♣) is the *lowest* suit, then come DIAMONDS (◇) and HEARTS (♡) to the highest ranking suit, SPADES (♠). NO TRUMPS ranks higher than any suit. The order of the suits – C, D, H, S – is no accident. They are in alphabetical order.

When selecting partnerships, if two cards of the same rank are chosen (e.g. two eights) and the tie needs to be broken, it is decided by suit order (e.g. the ◊ 8 would outrank the ♣ 8).

DEALING

The player who drew the highest card is the dealer on the first hand and has the right to choose seats and the pack of cards with which to deal. The next dealer is the player on dealer's left, and so on.

The cards are shuffled by the player on the dealer's left. The dealer passes the pack face down to the player on the dealer's right to be 'cut' (take some cards from the top of the pack; place them face down beside the pack). The dealer completes the cut, placing the rest of the pack on top of the cards cut. The dealer then deals the cards, one at a time, face down, in clockwise direction, starting with the player on the left, until all 52 cards are dealt, 13 cards to each player.

It is common courtesy to leave your cards face down until the dealer has finished dealing. A misdeal may be corrected if the players have not seen their cards. While the cards are dealt, the dealer's partner shuffles the other pack in preparation for the next deal. Two packs are used to speed up the game. After the shuffling is finished the cards are put down on the shuffler's right, ready for the next dealer to pick up.

THE START OF PLAY

When you pick up your 13 cards, sort them into suits. It is normal to separate the red suits and black suits so that you can easily see where one suit ends and the next suit begins. Most players find it easiest to arrange the cards with the highest cards in each suit on the left.

The bidding starts with the dealer. After the bidding period is over, the side that has bid higher wins the right to play the hand. One member of this side, called the declarer, plays the hand while the opponents defend the hand. The person on the left of the declarer plays a card face up on the table. This first card played is called the 'opening lead'. The partner of the declarer, called the dummy, now puts all 13 cards face up on the table and arranged in suits. The dummy takes no further part in the play, declarer playing both hands. Each player sees 26 cards, the 13 in hand plus the 13 in dummy.

Declarer plays one of the cards from dummy, then the third player plays a card and so does declarer. The four cards now face up on the table are called a 'trick'. A trick always consists of four cards played in clockwise sequence, one from each hand.

Each deal is a battle over thirteen tricks, declarer trying to win as many as nominated in the bidding, while the defenders try to win enough to defeat declarer. A trick is won by the highest card in the suit led or by the highest trump card. The player who wins a trick gathers the four cards together, puts them face down neatly and then leads to the next trick. Tricks for each partnership are usually gathered in one area, so that one can easily glance down and see how many tricks each side has won. Play continues until 13 tricks have been played. (In tournament bridge, called 'duplicate', the cards for each trick are not gathered together. Each player keeps his own cards in front of him.)

FOLLOWING SUIT

The basic rule of play is *you must follow suit*. You must play a card of the same suit as the suit led. If hearts are led, then you must play a heart if you have one and the trick is won by the highest heart played. Thus, if the 2 of hearts is led, and the other cards on the trick are the 10 of hearts, the queen of spades and the ace of clubs, the trick is won by the 10 of hearts. If you are unable to follow suit, you may play any other card at all, but remember it is the highest card of the first led suit which wins. If the king of spades is led, it will do you no good to play the ace of clubs – only the ace of spades beats the king of spades.

TRUMPS

There is one exception to this. Where one of the four suits is, in the bidding, made the *trump* suit, then any card in the trump suit is higher then any card, even an ace, in one of the other suits. So, if hearts are trumps, the 2 of hearts would beat the ace of clubs even when clubs are led. But, first and foremost, you must follow suit. Only when you are out of a suit can you beat a high card of another suit with a trump.

If you are unable to follow suit, you are allowed to 'ruff' (play a trump), *but it is not obligatory*. You may choose to discard. If partner has already won the trick, it may be foolish to ruff partner's winner.

A trick that does not contain a trump is won by the highest card in the suit led. A trick that contains a trump is won by the highest trump on the trick. If you fail to follow suit, when able to do so, you have 'revoked' (or 'reneged'). The penalty for a revoke is to transfer one or two tricks to the other side, one trick if your side does not win the revoke trick, two tricks if your side does win the revoke trick.

THE BIDDING

The play is preceded by the bidding, also called 'the auction'. Just as in an auction an item goes to the highest bidder, so in the bridge auction each side tries to outbid the other for the right to be declarer and play the hand.

The dealer makes the first bid, then the player on dealer's left and so on, in clockwise rotation. Each player may pass (say 'No Bid') or make a bid. A player who has previously passed may still make a bid later in the auction. A bid consists of a number (1, 2, 3, 4, 5, 6 or 7) followed by a suit or no trumps, e.g. 2 spades, 3 hearts, 4 no trumps, 7 diamonds. 'No trumps' means there is be no trump suit on the deal.

Whenever a bid is made, the bidder is stating the number of tricks *above six* intended to be won in the play. The minimum number of tricks for which you may bid is seven. A bid of 1 Club contracts to make seven tricks with clubs as trumps. The number in the bid is the number of tricks to be won *over and above six tricks*. (Six tricks is not even halfway and you have to bid for more than half the tricks to beat the other side.) The final bid is called the CONTRACT.

If all players pass without a bid on the first round, there is no play, there is no score, the cards are thrown in and the next dealer deals a new hand. When a player makes a bid on the first round, the auction has started and will be won by the side that bids higher. The auction continues, with each player making a bid or passing. The auction ends when a bid is followed by three passes.

The contract (the final bid) sets the trump suit (or no trumps) and the number of tricks to be won in the play. The side bidding the contract is the declarer side. The member of the declarer side who first bid the trump suit (or no trumps) is the declarer.

Each player in turn must pass or make a *higher* bid than the last bid. A bid is higher than the previous bid if it is a higher number than the previous bid, or the same number but in a higher ranking denomination. The order of ranking from the top is:

NO TRUMPS

SPADES

HEARTS

DIAMONDS

CLUBS

A bid of 1 Heart is higher than a bid of 1 Club. If you want to bid clubs and the previous bid was 2 Spades, you would have to bid 3 Clubs (or 4 Clubs or higher). 2 Clubs would not be higher than 2 Spades.

THE SCORING FOR GAMES AND RUBBER

A rubber of bridge is over when one side wins two games. A game is won by scoring 100 or more contract points when declarer.

It is vital to understand how the game is scored, for this affects both the bidding and the play. Your aim is to score more points than the opposition. You score points: (1) by bidding and making a contract as declarer (contract points, written below the line) or (2) by earning declarer bonus points or defender bonus points (written above the line).

After the 13 tricks have been played, the number of tricks won by each side is agreed and the score calculated. A scoresheet looks like this:

WE	THEY
Bonus	Points
Contract	Points

Contract Points: If declarer has made the contract, the score for the contract is written below the line. Contract points are:

1NT = 40, plus 30 for each additional trick at no trumps.

Spades or hearts as trumps: 30 each.

Diamonds or clubs as trumps: 20 each.

Multiply the above values by 2 if the contract is doubled and by 4 if the contract is redoubled.

If you have not scored any contract points, a contract of 5 Clubs or 5 Diamonds is needed to make game in the minors, while a contract of 4 Hearts or 4 Spades or more will score game in the majors. For no trumps, a bid of 3 No Trumps will score a game.

The declaring side gets credit not for the tricks won but only for the tricks bid and then won. So if 4 ♡ is bid, and declarer makes 9 tricks, declarer does not get credit for 9 tricks but suffers a penalty for failing to make the contract by one trick. Thus accuracy in bidding distinguishes contract bridge from auction bridge (where you are given credit for what you make, even if you did not bid it) and becomes the single most important element in the game's winning strategy.

Only points scored by winning the actual number of tricks of the contract are written below the line and only contract points below the line count towards winning games and the rubber.

A score below the line of less than 100 is called a *partscore*. You may combine two or more partscores to score the 100 points for game. You cannot carry forward any points over and above 100 to the next game. After one side scores a game, a line is drawn across both columns and both sides start from zero for the next game. So, if you have a partscore but the enemy score a game before you have been able to convert your partscore into a game, you have to start from zero for the next game . . . they have *underlined* you.

DOUBLES AND REDOUBLES

In the bidding, any player may at his turn double a bid made by an opponent. Say 'Double'. If there is no further bidding, the double increases the rewards for success and the penalties for failure. After a double, the other side may redouble (say 'Redouble'), increasing the rewards and penalties further.

Any double or redouble is cancelled by a later bid, but there may be further doubles and redoubles of later bids. 1 ♠ making 7 tricks scores 30 contract points, but 1 ♠ doubled making 7 tricks scores 60 contract points, while 1 ♠ doubled and redoubled and making 7 tricks scores 120 contract points (and game!). In each instance there are 50 bonus points for making a doubled contract ('for the insult').

Each side may score bonus points written *above the line*. There is a complete scoring table on page 42 to which you can refer after each deal is over. You need to memorise only the trick value of each suit and no trumps. You will soon be familiar with the common bonus scores and the other scoring will be learned gradually as you play.

DECLARER BONUS POINTS:

Overtricks: For each trick made above the contract, the same trick value as for contract points (NT = 30, ♠/♡ = 30, ♢/♣ = 20)

For a small slam (bidding 6 and making 12 tricks):

+500 when not vulnerable, +750 when vulnerable

For a grand slam (bidding 7 and making 13 tricks):

+1000 when not vulnerable, +1500 when vulnerable

Vulnerable = Having won one game.

Not vulnerable = Not having won one game.

For winning Game 1 in a rubber: +350

For winning Game 2 in a rubber: +350

For winning Games 3 in a rubber (if the game score is 1-1): +500

    The above scores are often added at the end of a rubber (+700 for a 2-0 win, +500 for a 2-1 win), but for beginners and especially children, it is more instructive to add the bonus for each game as soon as a game is won. This clearly demonstrates value of bidding and making games (and the ultimate score comes out exactly the same).

    For doubled or redoubled overtricks and other bonuses, see page 42.

DEFENDERS' BONUS POINTS

Defenders can score only bonus points, not contract points. Where declarer fails to make the contract, the defenders score:

If declarer is not vulnerable: 50 points for each trick by which declarer fell short. If the contract was doubled, 100 points for one down and 200 for every extra down trick. This increases to 200 and 400 if redoubled.

If declarer is vulnerable: 100 points for each trick by which declarer fell short. If the contract was doubled, this becomes 200 points for one down and 300 for every extra down trick. This increases to 400 and 600 if the contract was redoubled.

Note that the bonus points for defeating a contract are the same regardless of the contract. One down in 2♡ produces the same score as one down in 7NT.

BONUSES FOR HONOURS

At rubber bridge there are rewards for being lucky enough to hold certain honour cards (the honours are the A, K, Q, J and 10 in each suit). You score 150 for holding all 5 trump honours in one hand or 100 points for any 4 trump honours in one hand. You can also score 150 points for holding 4 aces in one hand if the contract is no trumps. Bonuses for honours are scored whether or not the contract is made. The bonuses are available if the required honours are held by declarer, by dummy or by either defender. In order not to give away to the opponents the fact that you hold good cards, the honours' bonus is usually claimed only after the play of a deal has been completed. Honours cannot be claimed once play on the next deal has started. Honours are not scored when playing duplicate.

When the rubber ends, add up all the points in each column, bonus points and contract points. The side with more points is the winner. Subtract the loser's score from the winner's and round it off to the nearest hundred (50 goes down, not up). The score is kept in hundreds (+11 means having won a rubber of 1100, −8 means having lost a rubber of 800). This is the margin of victory and the score for the rubber for each player.

For complete details for scoring, check page 42.

Chapter 7

Valuing Your Hand

To work out the strength of your hand, add up these points:

HIGH CARD POINTS (HCP)

$$A = 4 \qquad K = 3 \qquad Q = 2 \qquad J = 1$$

LENGTH POINTS (LP)

For a 5-card suit: Add 1 point for each 5-card suit
For a 6-card suit: Add 2 points
For a 7-card suit: Add 3 points

All bidding, all hand valuation and all play is about winning tricks. We measure the number of tricks we are likely to win by counting points. The number of points you and partner have together indicates the number of tricks you probably will win in no trumps or your agreed trump suit. The more points, the more tricks. We count points for the good features in a hand, the cards that are likely to win tricks. We count points for HIGH CARDS, LENGTH CARDS and TRUMP CARDS.

The HIGH CARDS are the top four cards in each suit, the aces, kings, queens and jacks. These are the cards most likely to win tricks on the first rounds of a suit.

The LENGTH CARDS are the excess cards in a long suit, the fifth, the sixth and any extra cards. After four rounds of a suit, it is unlikely that an opponent will still have cards left in this suit, so there is a good chance that your extra cards will be winners.

The TRUMP CARDS are low cards that can win tricks by ruffing. You will not know about trump cards until you and partner have agreed on a trump suit. Points for high cards and length cards can be worked out as soon as you have sorted your cards out, but points for trump cards are not counted until later, when a trump suit is agreed.

EXERCISES

How many points are these hands worth? Count HCP + LP. Work
out your own answers before checking the answers below.

1. ♠ K J 5
   ♡ A 9 8 3 2
   ◇ 9 8 6 2
   ♣ A

2. ♠ A K 9 4 2
   ♡ A Q J 9 2
   ◇ 5
   ♣ K Q

3. ♠ 8 7 4 3 2
   ♡ A K Q J
   ◇ Q J 7 4
   ♣ - - -

4. ♠ 10 8
   ♡ Q 9 2
   ◇ A J
   ♣ A K J 6 5 3

5. ♠ Q 9 5
   ♡ A J 8 3
   ◇ K 6 2
   ♣ Q 7 2

6. ♠ A K 9 4
   ♡ Q J 2
   ◇ 5 3
   ♣ K Q 8 6

7. ♠ 10 8 6 2
   ♡ A Q J
   ◇ K Q 5
   ♣ A K J

8. ♠ A 4
   ♡ K Q J 7 5 3 2
   ◇ 9
   ♣ 6 5 3

9. ♠ A K J 5
   ♡ 3
   ◇ K J 9 2
   ♣ A Q 8 7

10. ♠ A K J 5 2
    ♡ - - -
    ◇ K J 9
    ♣ A Q 8 7 2

11. ♠ A 6
    ♡ A K 9 8 5 2
    ◇ 7 4
    ♣ 9 8 2

12. ♠ A J 8 7 4 3
    ♡ 2
    ◇ A J 10 6 2
    ♣ 5

Answers to Exercises:

1. 13 (1 LP)
2. 21 (2 LP)
3. 14 (1 LP)
4. 17 (2 LP)
5. 12 (0 LP)
6. 15 (0 LP)
7. 20 (0 LP)
8. 13 (3 LP)
9. 18 (0 LP)
10 20 (2 LP)
11. 13 (2 LP)
12. 13 (3 LP)

Chapter 8

Bidding Strategy

These are the key points for judging your bidding level:

37 points or more:
BID A GRAND SLAM
(A grand slam is a bid of 7♣, 7♢, 7♡, 7♠ or 7NT)

33 points or more:
BID A SMALL SLAM
(A small slam is a bid of 6♣, 6♢, 6♡, 6♠ or 6NT)

25 points or more:
BID A GAME
(A game contract is a bid of 3NT, 4♡, 4♠, 5♣ or 5♢)

Under 25 points:
STOP AS LOW AS YOU CAN, AT THE 2-LEVEL OR
LOWER IF POSSIBLE

Because there are such big bonuses for games and slams, the most important contracts are the game contracts, those that give you 100 or more points in one go (3NT, 4♡, 4♠, 5♣, 5♢) and slam contracts (6-level and 7-level bids). To make a game, you need 26 points or something close to it. 26 points gives a very good chance to make a game, but even with 25 points, you have a good chance. Because the rewards for game are great, be prepared to take your chances and bid game if you are sure the partnership has at least 25 points. For a small slam, you need about 33 points and for a grand slam, about 37 points.

If you can make a game but fail to bid it, you have missed out on a valuable bonus for the game. It is better to bid games, and fail now and then, than to stop lower and not score the bonus for a game that can be made. If a slam is available but you do not bid it, again you miss out on a substantial bonus (500 points or more). Judging when to bid games and slams and when to stop at a lower contract is the challenge and the excitement of the bidding.

EXERCISE

A. Partner has shown a hand suitable for no trumps and 12-14 points. Your hand is also suitable for no trumps. How high would you want to bid if you hold the number of points given below?

1. 9	2. 13	3. 17	4. 22
5. 15	6. 26	7. 10	8. 6

B. Partner has shown a hand suitable for no trumps and 20-22 points. Your hand is also suitable for no trumps. How high would you want to bid if you hold the number of points given below?

1. 7	2. 2	3. 13	4. 20

C. You know that your partnership has a very strong trump suit in hearts. Partner has bid 2♡ and shown 6-9 points. How high would you wish to bid if you hold the number of points given below?

1. 13	2. 15	3. 19	4. 21

Answers to Exercise:

A.   1. 1NT   2. 3NT   3. 3NT   4. 6NT
      5. 3NT   6. 7NT   7. 1NT   8. 1NT

B.   1. 3NT   2. 2NT   3. 6NT   4. 7NT

C.   1. 2♡   2. 2♡   3. 4♡   4. 4♡

Chapter 9

Point Count Zones, Balanced Hands And Unbalanced Hands

To play in a trump contract at a high level (4 or higher) you should hold at least eight trumps between you and partner or have a long, powerful suit of your own. At lower levels, it is still desirable to have at least 8 trumps together but you might survive with only 7 trumps. Never choose a trump suit where you and partner hold only 6 trumps or fewer (since the opponents hold 7 and so they are more likely to succeed).

This table indicates the number of tricks you are likely to win at a trump contract for various point ranges:

For a suit contract at the 2-level – 8 tricks	: 19-21 points
For a suit contract at the 3-level – 9 tricks	: 22-24 points
For a suit contract at the 4-level – 10 tricks	: 25-28 points
For a suit contract at the 5-level – 11 tricks	: 29-32 points
For a suit contract at the 6-level – 12 tricks	: 33-36 points
For a suit contract at the 7-level – 13 tricks	: 37-40 points

No trump contracts are best when the partnership hands are balanced (see next page) or when it turns out that there is no trump suit in which the partnership holds at least eight trumps. This table indicates the number of tricks the partnership is likely to win at no trumps for various point ranges:

For a contract of 1NT – 7 tricks	: 19-21 points
For a contract of 2NT – 8 tricks	: 22-24 points
For a contract of 3NT – 9 tricks	: 25 points or more
For a contract of 6NT – 12 tricks	: 33 points or more
For a contract of 7NT – 13 tricks	: 37 points or more

UNBALANCED HANDS

> Void   = No cards in a suit
> Singleton   = One card in a suit
> Doubleton = Two cards in a suit

An unbalanced hand is any hand which contains a void or a singleton. An unbalanced hand is best for a trump contract because it is easy to score tricks by ruffing the suit where you are short. If opening the bidding with an unbalanced hand, always start with a suit bid.

BALANCED HANDS

A balanced hand contains no void and no singleton. The balanced patterns are **4-3-3-3**, **4-4-3-2** and **5-3-3-2**. (4-3-3-3 means you have one 4-card suit and three 3-card suits, 4-4-3-2 means you have two 4-card suits, one 3-card suit and one doubleton, and so on.) These balanced patterns have at most one doubleton. Balanced hands often play best in no trumps because there is no short suit which you can ruff quickly. If opening the bidding with a balanced hand, start with a no trump bid or, if this is not possible (see next chapter), try to bid no trumps with your second bid.

SEMI-BALANCED HANDS

Hands which contain two or three doubletons (the 5-4-2-2, 6-3-2-2 or 7-2-2-2 patterns) are called 'semi-balanced'. They are good for a trump contract if the partnership holds 8 or more trumps. If not, they are still reasonable for no trumps because there is no singleton or void. If opening the bidding with a semi-balanced hand, start with a suit bid.

EXERCISE

Are these hands balanced, unbalanced or semi-balanced?

1. ♠ K Q 6	2. ♠ A K 9 4 2	3. ♠ A 8 7 4 3 2
♡ Q 8 6	♡ A 2	♡ J
◊ J 6 4 3 2	◊ K Q 3 2	◊ Q J 7 4
♣ A J	♣ 8 5	♣ A J

Answers: 1. Balanced   2. Semi-balanced   3. Unbalanced

Chapter 10

Opening The Bidding

A pass does not count as a bid and the first (positive) bid made is called the 'opening bid'. The requirements for an opening bid are higher than for later bids. The player making the first bid is called the 'opener'. The partner of the opener is the 'responder' and the opponents are the 'defenders'.

OPENING THE BIDDING WITH A BALANCED HAND

0-11 HCP :   Pass. Do not open the bidding. You may bid later.
12-14 HCP :   Open 1NT. This shows your strength and shape.
20-22 HCP :   Open 2NT. This shows your strength and shape.
15-19 HCP :   Open with a suit bid. You can bid no trumps later.
A suit bid promises four or more cards in that suit. With only one 4-card suit (the 4-3-3-3 pattern) or one 5-card suit (5-3-3-2 pattern), you have no choice. Bid your longest suit. If you have two 4-card suits (the 4-4-3-2 pattern), bid your lowest ranking 4-card suit. (Spades is the highest ranking suit, then come hearts followed by diamonds, and clubs is the lowest ranking suit.)
23 points up :   Open 2♣. To start 2♣ is a message to partner that you hold a powerful hand, at least 23 points. Partner is obliged to reply to your 2♣ opening. This is covered in Chapter 14.

HANDS THAT ARE NOT BALANCED

With an unbalanced or a semi-balanced hand, open the bidding with 12 HCP or more (or 13 points or more counting HCP + LP), but pass with fewer points. You may still bid later. With enough to open:
(a) Open with your longer suit first.
(b) With two 5-card suits, open the higher ranking suit.

The 4-4-4-1 pattern is a special case. With a red singleton, open the suit below the singleton (with a diamond singleton, open 1 ♣; with a heart singleton, open 1 ◇). With a black singleton, open the middle suit (with a club singleton, open 1 ♡; with a spade singleton, open 1 ◇).

EXERCISES

For each of these hands:
  (a) How many points does it contain?
  (b) Is it balanced, unbalanced or semi-balanced?
  (c) What is your opening bid?

1. ♠ K J 5	2. ♠ K J 5 3	3. ♠ K J 4 3 2
♡ A 9 8 2	♡ A 9 8 2	♡ A K Q 7 2
◇ 9 8 6 2	◇ A 8 6 2	◇ 7 4
♣ A 3	♣ 7	♣ 2

4. ♠ A Q	5. ♠ A J 5	6. ♠ A K Q 7
♡ K Q 9 2	♡ A J 3	♡ A Q
◇ J 7 4	◇ K Q 2	◇ 8 7
♣ A 6 5 3	♣ A Q 5 2	♣ 6 5 4 3 2

7. ♠ Q J 2	8. ♠ 4	9. ♠ A K J 5
♡ A K 9 4	♡ K Q 8 7 5 3 2	♡ 3
◇ A K	◇ A 9	◇ Q J 9 2
♣ A Q J 3	♣ Q 5 3	♣ A J 5 3

Answers to Exercises:

1. 12, bal: 1 NT	2. 12, unbal; 1 ♡	3. 15, unbal; 1 ♠
4. 16, bal: 1 ♣	5. 21, bal; 2 NT	6. 16, semi-bal; 1 ♣
7. 24, bal: 2 ♣	8. 14, unbal; 1 ♡	9. 16, unbal; 1 ◇

Chapter 11

Responder's Actions

RESPONDING TO 1NT

Your actions are based on two questions 'Do we have enough for a game (25 points or more)?' and 'Do we have enough for a slam?' With a balanced hand, this is how you respond:

0-10 : Pass	13-18 : 3NT	21-24 : 6NT
11-12 : 2NT	19-20 : 4NT	25-28 : 7NT

After 1NT : 2NT, opener passes with 12 points and bids on with 13-14. After 1NT : 4NT, opener passes with 12 points and bids on with more.

When you know you have at least eight trumps, count only HCP plus Trump Points as follows (do not count Length Points as well):

$$VOID = 5 \quad SINGLETON = 3 \quad DOUBLETON = 1$$

With a hand that is not balanced and no chance for game, bid your long suit (at least a 5-card suit) at the 2-level (e.g. 1NT : 2♠). Opener is expected to pass your 2-level suit response. With enough for game and a 5-card suit, bid your suit at the 3-level (e.g. 1NT : 3 ♠). Opener will raise your suit (1NT : 3♠, 4♠) with three or four trumps and will bid 3NT (1NT : 3♠, 3NT) with only a doubleton in your suit. With a 6-card or longer major and enough for a game, you can bid game in your suit at once (1NT : 4♠ or 1NT : 4♡) as opener will have two or more trumps. The 1NT opening cannot be unbalanced and so cannot have a singleton.

RESPONDING TO 2NT

With a balanced hand, add your points to opener's 20-22 and then –

0-2 : Pass   3-10 : 3NT   11-12 : 4NT   13-16 : 6NT   17-20 : 7NT

With an unbalanced hand and enough for game (3 points or more), bid your long suit at the 3-level (at least a 5-card suit, e.g. 2NT : 3♡). With a 6-card or longer major and enough for game, you may bid game in your major at once (e.g. 2NT : 4♡). The 2NT opening is balanced and guarantees at least doubleton support.

EXERCISES

Partner has opened 1NT. What is your reply on each of these hands?

1. ♠ K J 5
   ♡ A 9 8
   ◇ A 8 6 2
   ♣ A 3 2

2. ♠ K Q J 5 3
   ♡ 2
   ◇ A 8 6 2
   ♣ Q 9 7

3. ♠ A K J 4 3 2
   ♡ K 6 4
   ◇ - - -
   ♣ 5 4 3 2

4. ♠ A Q 3
   ♡ K Q 9
   ◇ A 7 4
   ♣ A K 5 3

5. ♠ J 7 6
   ♡ J
   ◇ Q J 8 6 4 2
   ♣ Q 5 2

6. ♠ J 7 3
   ♡ A Q
   ◇ K 8 7 5
   ♣ Q 10 5 2

Partner has opened 2NT. What is your reply on each of these hands?

7. ♠ J 9 5
   ♡ 7 4 2
   ◇ 8 7 5
   ♣ 9 8 6 2

8. ♠ 5 3
   ♡ Q J 8 7 3 2
   ◇ 2
   ♣ 9 7 4 3

9. ♠ A K J
   ♡ Q J 2
   ◇ Q 9 6
   ♣ J 8 7 2

10. ♠ A 10 3
    ♡ 8 5
    ◇ 9 7 4
    ♣ J 6 5 3 2

11. ♠ 5
    ♡ 7
    ◇ J 8 6 4
    ♣ Q 8 7 6 5 3 2

12. ♠ A 9 7 5 3
    ♡ 9 2
    ◇ K 8 7 5
    ♣ 5 2

Answers to Exercises:

1. 3 NT

2. 3 ♠

3. 4 ♠

4. 6 NT

5. 2 ◇

6. 2 NT

7. No bid

8. 4 ♡

9. 6 NT

10. 3 NT

11. 5 ♣

12. 3 ♠

RESPONDING TO A SUIT OPENING AT THE 1-LEVEL

The normal requirement for a response is 6 points or better, but many players will reply with a 5-point hand rather than let the bidding die out at the 1-level and rather than let the opposition in cheaply. The possible actions are a raise of opener's suit, a change to another suit or a response in no trumps. You should treat a bid only as a suggestion. If that suggestion does not suit your hand, make some other suggestion (bid something else).

RESPONDING IN NO TRUMPS

1NT = 6-9 points   **2NT** = 10-12 points   **3NT** = 13-15 points
Count only HCP when responding in no trumps. Opener is permitted to pass any no trump response.

RAISING OPENER'S SUIT

2-level = 6-9 points   **3-level** = 10-12 points   **4-level** = 13-15 points
When supporting opener's suit, count HCP plus Trumps Points (5 for a void, 3 for a singleton, 1 for a doubleton). Do not count Length Points as well. Opener is permitted to pass any raise.

BIDDING A NEW SUIT

1. At the 1-level in a higher-ranking suit (e.g. 1◇ : 1♠)
This shows **6-15 points** and at least a 4-card suit. Opener is not permitted to pass a new suit reply. The principle is known as 'change of suit by responder is forcing'. With a no trumps response or a raise response, responder has already indicated whether the range is 6-9, 10-12 or 13-15. With a new suit response, responder needs a second bid to clarify whether the hand is 6-9, 10-12 or 13-15. Therefore, opener must rebid to give responder that second chance.

2. At the 2-level in a lower-ranking suit (e.g. 1♠ : 2◇)
This shows at least a 4-card suit and **10-15 points**. Opener is not permitted to pass a change of suit reply so that responder will be able to clarify later whether the range is 10-12 or 13-15.

3. The jump shift (e.g. 1♣ : 2♡ or 1♠ : 3♣)
This shows **16 points or more** and is forcing to game. Both players keep bidding until game or slam has been reached.

EXERCISES

A. Partner has opened 1 ◇. What is your response?

1. ♠ 8 5 4
   ♡ A J 8
   ◇ 8 6 2
   ♣ K 5 4 2

2. ♠ A 8 6
   ♡ K 9 2
   ◇ K 7 5
   ♣ J 9 8 2

3. ♠ K 5
   ♡ 8 7 6
   ◇ A 9 7 4
   ♣ 8 5 4 2

4. ♠ A 10 8
   ♡ 9 5 3
   ◇ A K 5 3
   ♣ 9 8 5

5. ♠ Q J 9 5
   ♡ K 7 5 2
   ◇ 2
   ♣ A 9 8 3

6. ♠ A Q J 5 3
   ♡ - - -
   ◇ 8 7 2
   ♣ Q 8 7 6 3

7. ♠ A J 9
   ♡ A J 8
   ◇ Q 8 5 2
   ♣ K 8 6

8. ♠ A 8 4 3
   ♡ 5 2
   ◇ Q 9 6 2
   ♣ 9 8 7

9. ♠ A 5
   ♡ 8 3 2
   ◇ K J 2
   ♣ K 9 7 5 2

10. ♠ 2
    ♡ K 7 5 2
    ◇ K 8 7 4
    ♣ 9 7 4 2

11. ♠ 2
    ♡ K 7 5 2
    ◇ K 8 7 4
    ♣ A 9 7 4

12. ♠ J 4
    ♡ Q 7 6 4 2
    ◇ 5
    ♣ A K Q 3 2

B. What would your responses have been if partner had opened 1 ♠?

Answers to Exercise A:

1. 1 NT
2. 2 NT
3. 2 ◇

4. 3 ◇
5. 1 ♡
6. 1 ♠

7. 3 NT
8. 1 ♠
9. 2 ♣

10. 1 ♡
11. 1 ♡
12. 1 ♡

Answers to Exercise B:

1. 1 NT
2. 2 NT
3. 1 NT

4. 2 ◇
5. 4 ♠
6. 4 ♠

7. 3 NT
8. 2 ♠
9. 2 ♣

10. 1 NT
11. 2 ♣
12. 2 ♡

CHOICE OF RESPONSES

Often you may have a choice of action when responding. These guidelines will help you to choose the best response.

If you hold 6-9 points and partner opened 1♣ or 1◇:

1. *Change suit at the 1-level.* When changing suit, follow the rule: Longest suit first, higher with 5-card suits, cheapest with 4-card suits.

2. *Raise partner's minor to the 2-level.* You need 4 trumps to support.

3. *Respond 1NT.* The 1NT response is the least attractive choice.

If you hold 6-9 points and partner opened 1♡ or 1♠:

1. *Raise partner's major to the 2-level.* You should have 4 trumps to support. (Exception: Raise also with 3 trumps plus a singleton or a void.)

2. *Bid 1 Spade over 1 Heart.* You need at least 4 cards in spades.

3. *Respond 1NT.* Again, 1NT is the last resort. Prefer anything else reasonable, but avoid changing suit to the 2-level with only 6-9 points.

If you hold 10-12 points:

1. *Raise opener's major suit opening to the 3-level.* The No. 1 choice. You need at least four trumps for this jump raise (e.g. 1♠ : 3♠).

2. *Change suit at the 1-level or the 2-level.* Later, rebid 2NT or support opener's suit at the 3-level or rebid your own suit at the 3-level.

3. *Respond 2NT.* No void, no singleton, no long suit.

4. *Raise opener's minor suit opening to the 3-level.* You need at least four trumps. Prefer to change suit or respond 2NT if possible.

If you hold 13-15 points:

1. *Raise opener's major suit opening to the 4-level.*

2. *Change suit at the 1-level or 2-level.* Later, rebid 3NT or bid game in opener's suit or in your own suit or change suit again.

3. *Respond 3NT.* No void, no singleton, no long suit.

4. *Raise opener's minor suit opening to the 4-level.* Only in desperation.

If you hold 16 points or more:

Choose a jump shift (e.g. 1♣ : 2♡) in your longest suit. If your suits are of equal length, jump in the higher with two 5-card suits or in the cheapest with 4-card suits. After the jump shift, responder should rebid game with just 16-19 points and bid a slam with 20 or more.

EXERCISES

A. Partner has opened 1♣. What is your response?

1. ♠ K J 5
   ♡ A 9 8 3 2
   ◇ Q 8 6 2
   ♣ 6

2. ♠ A K 9 4
   ♡ Q J 9 2
   ◇ 8 7 5
   ♣ 7 2

3. ♠ 5
   ♡ 8 7 6 4 3 2
   ◇ A Q 9 7 4
   ♣ 4

4. ♠ K 10 8
   ♡ Q 9 3
   ◇ Q 7 5 3
   ♣ 9 8 5

5. ♠ J 9 5
   ♡ 5 2
   ◇ K 6 2
   ♣ A Q 9 7 2

6. ♠ A Q J 5
   ♡ Q J 2
   ◇ K 8 7
   ♣ Q 7 6

7. ♠ A J 9 6 2
   ♡ A Q J 2
   ◇ K Q 2
   ♣ 6

8. ♠ A 4
   ♡ Q J 7 5
   ◇ 9 2
   ♣ Q 8 6 5 3

9. ♠ A 5
   ♡ 8 3 2
   ◇ A K J 2
   ♣ A K 9 7

10. ♠ A K J 5 2
    ♡ - - -
    ◇ K J 9 6 5
    ♣ 8 6 5

11. ♠ A K J 5 2
    ♡ - - -
    ◇ A K 9 6 5
    ♣ K 8 2

12. ♠ A Q J 4
    ♡ 2
    ◇ A J 10 6 2
    ♣ 5 3 2

B. What would your responses have been if partner had opened 1♡?

Answers to Exercise A:

1. 1 ♡
2. 1 ♡
3. 1 ♡

4. 1 ◇
5. 3 ♣
6. 1 ♠

7. 2 ♠
8. 1 ♡
9. 2 ◇

10. 1 ♠
11. 2 ♠
12. 1 ◇

Answers to Exercise B:

1. 4 ♡
2. 3 ♡
3. 4 ♡

4. 1 NT
5. 2 ♣
6. 1 ♠

7. 2 ♠
8. 3 ♡
9. 3 ♣

10. 1 ♠
11. 2 ♠
12. 2 ◇

Chapter 12

Opener's Rebid

AFTER A RAISE

If responder raised your major, stay with the major. Revalue your hand by adding HCP plus Trump Points (5 for a void, 3 for a singleton, 1 for a doubleton). Do not count Length Points as well. Pass if you cannot have at least 25 points together. Bid on if 25 or more points are possible and bid game if 25 or more points are a certainty.

If responder raised your minor, pass without 25 points together. With 25 points or more possible or certain, bid on. Strongly consider rebidding into no trumps when there are game chances rather than trying for the 5-level in your minor.

AFTER A NO TRUMPS RESPONSE

If your hand is balanced stay with no trumps. Pass if the combined points are below 25 but bid on if game points are possible or certain. If your hand is not balanced, change suit if you hold a second suit or repeat your suit if you have only one long suit. With a weak hand, bid the suit at the cheapest level. With chances for games, make a jump bid.

AFTER A CHANGE OF SUIT RESPONSE

Opener must not pass. Follow this order of priorities:

1. Raise responder's suit. When raising partner, count HCP plus Trump Points.

2. Change suit or rebid no trumps with a balanced hand. A NT rebid is 15-16 points at the cheapest level. 17 or more for a jump rebid.

3. Repeat your own suit. To repeat your first suit, the suit must contain at least five cards. However, repeating your suit is the last resort. Try to take some other action if possible. Do not repeat your suit if you can support partner's suit.

Rebid at the cheapest level with a minimum opening (12-15 points). A jump rebid by opener shows a minimum of 16 points.

EXERCISES

A. You opened 1 ◇ and partner responded 1 ♡. What is your rebid?

1. ♠ J 5
   ♡ A 9 8 4
   ◇ A Q J 3 2
   ♣ 6 4

2. ♠ A 8 6 2
   ♡ 9
   ◇ K Q 7 5
   ♣ A 9 8 2

3. ♠ K Q 3
   ♡ 8 7 6
   ◇ A 9 7 4
   ♣ A Q 2

4. ♠ A Q 8
   ♡ Q 5 3
   ◇ A K 5 3
   ♣ K J 5

5. ♠ 5 2
   ♡ Q 7
   ◇ A K J 8 7
   ♣ A 9 8 3

6. ♠ A 9 7
   ♡ A Q 8 4
   ◇ A K J 7 5
   ♣ 7

7. ♠ K J 9
   ♡ A 7
   ◇ K Q 8 6 5 2
   ♣ 8 2

8. ♠ K Q
   ♡ A J
   ◇ A Q J 6 5 2
   ♣ 8 6 2

9. ♠ K Q 6 5 3
   ♡ 2
   ◇ A K J 8 7 2
   ♣ 4

10. ♠ 2
    ♡ K Q 7 5
    ◇ K 8 7 6
    ♣ A K 4 2

11. ♠ 2
    ♡ K 7 5 2
    ◇ A K Q 8 7 4
    ♣ A 9

12. ♠ 7 4
    ♡ K J 9 4
    ◇ A K Q 8
    ♣ K Q J

B. What would your rebid have been if partner had responded 1NT?

Answer to Exercise A:

1. 2 ♡	2. 1 ♠	3. 1 NT
4. 3 NT	5. 2 ♣	6. 4 ♡
7. 2 ◇	8. 3 ◇	9. 1 ♠
10. 3 ♡	11. 4 ♡	12. 4 ♡

Answers to Exercise B:

1. 2 ◇	2. 2 ♣	3. No bid
4. 3 NT	5. 2 ♣	6. 2 ♡
7. 2 ◇	8. 3 ◇	9. 2 ♠
10. 2 ♣	11. 2 ♡	12. 3 NT

Chapter 13

Responder's Rebid

AFTER A RAISE

If opener raised your major, stay with the major. Revalue your hand by adding HCP plus Trump Points (5 for a void, 3 for a singleton, 1 for a doubleton). Do not count Length Points as well. Pass if you cannot have at least 25 points together. Bid on if 25 or more points are possible and bid game if 25 or more points are a certainty.

If opener raised your minor, pass without 25 points together. With 25 points or more possible or certain, bid on. Strongly consider rebidding into no trumps when there are game chances rather than trying for the 5-level in your minor.

AFTER A NO TRUMPS REBID

If your hand is balanced stay with no trumps. Pass if the combined points are below 25 but bid on if game points are possible or certain. If your hand is not balanced, change suit if you hold a second suit or repeat your suit if you have only one long suit. With a weak hand, bid the suit at the cheapest level. With chances for game, make a jump bid.

AFTER A CHANGE OF SUIT RESPONSE

Responder is permitted to pass unless opener's second bid was a jump shift. After a simple change of suit by opener, responder should follow this order of priorities:

1. 6-9 points: Rebid 1NT or a suit at the 2-level. Prefer to support one of opener's suits to rebidding a 5-card suit of your own.

2. 10-12 points: Rebid 2NT or a suit at the 3-level or change suit at the 2-level. Support one of opener's suits if possible.

3. 13-15 points: Rebid in some game contract if you know the best spot. If you have enough points for game but are still not sure of the best contract, change suit again. A change of suit by responder over opener's suit rebid is still forcing.

EXERCISES

Partner: 1◇, You: 1♡, Partner: 1♠. Your rebid?

1. ♠ K J 5
   ♡ K 9 8 2
   ◇ 8 6 2
   ♣ Q 3 2

2. ♠ K Q 8 5
   ♡ Q J 9 2
   ◇ 6 2
   ♣ 10 7 6

3. ♠ J 4
   ♡ K J 9 6 4
   ◇ Q 8 7 2
   ♣ 7 2

4. ♠ 8 6 3
   ♡ Q 8 6 4
   ◇ Q J 4
   ♣ A K 5

5. ♠ K J 7 6
   ♡ A J 8 6 3
   ◇ J 2
   ♣ 5 2

6. ♠ Q 7 3
   ♡ A Q 7 5
   ◇ K 8 7 5
   ♣ 5 2

Partner: 1♡, You: 1♠, Partner: 2◇. Your rebid?

7. ♠ A J 9 5 4
   ♡ 7 4
   ◇ 8 7 5 2
   ♣ J 2

8. ♠ A Q 5 3
   ♡ J 8 7
   ◇ 6 2
   ♣ 9 7 4 3

9. ♠ A K J 10 7 5
   ♡ Q 2
   ◇ 9 7 6
   ♣ 4 3

10. ♠ A Q 10 3
    ♡ 8 5
    ◇ 9 7 4
    ♣ A J 5 3

11. ♠ K J 7 5
    ♡ Q 4 2
    ◇ A J 6
    ♣ 5 3 2

12. ♠ A K 7 5
    ♡ 6 2
    ◇ K 8 3
    ♣ A J 5 2

Answers to Exercises:

1. 1 NT

2. 2 ♠

3. 2 ◇

4. 2 NT

5. 3 ♠

6. 3 ◇

7. No bid

8. 2 ♡

9. 3 ♠

10. 2 NT

11. 3 ♡

12. 3 NT

Chapter 14

Opening 2♣, 2◇, 2♡, 2♠

THE 2♣ OPENING

The 2♣ opening shows either a hand of 23 HCP or more or a hand with fewer points but enough tricks for a game. Open 2♣ with:

♠ A Q 9	♠ A Q J 10 7	♠ K Q J 7 6
♡ K J 10	♡ A K Q J 9	♡ - - -
◇ A K Q 8	◇ A 9	◇ A K Q J 7 2
♣ A 8 7	♣ 2	♣ A 5

The 2♣ opening is forcing. With a poor hand (less than 8 HCP), responder bids 2◇ and opener then bids the long suit or no trumps. After 2♣ : 2◇, 2NT (which shows 23-24 points and a balanced hand), responder may pass. After any rebid other than 2NT, the bidding must keep going until game or slam is reached.

With a good hand, responder makes any bid other than 2◇. Bid your longest suit or, if balanced, respond 2NT. A strong responding hand is one with any 8 HCP, or 7 HCP consisting of an ace and a king. A strong response is forcing to game and suggests slam is likely.

THE 2◇, 2♡ AND 2♠ OPENINGS

These promise a good 5-card or longer suit and a hand worth about 8-9 tricks, about one trick weaker than a 2♣ opening. Game is likely if partner can produce one useful high card. These hands are suitable:

♠ A Q J	♠ A 7	♠ K Q J 9 7 6
♡ K J 10 9 8 4	♡ A 9	♡ 8
◇ A K Q	◇ A K Q 8 7 4 3	◇ A K Q J 7
♣ 7	♣ J 2	♣ 5
Open 2♡	Open 2◇	Open 2♠

These openings are forcing for one round. If weak, respond 2NT. With better than one sure winner, support opener's suit or bid your own suit or bid 3NT. A response other than 2NT is forcing to game.

EXERCISES

Partner opened 2♣. What is your response?

1. ♠ 9 8 5	2. ♠ Q 8 5	3. ♠ J 4
♡ 10 9 8 2	♡ Q 10 9 2	♡ K J 9
◇ 8	◇ 6	◇ Q 8 7 5
♣ 9 8 6 4 3	♣ A J 10 7 6	♣ K 6 5 2

You opened 2♣ and partner replied 2◇. Your rebid?

4. ♠ A K 8 6	5. ♠ K 9 7	6. ♠ A Q J 6 3
♡ A Q	♡ A J 8	♡ 7 5
◇ J 9	◇ A K Q	◇ A K Q J 4
♣ A K Q J 5	♣ A K Q 2	♣ A

Partner: 2♣, You: 2◇, Partner: 2♠. Your rebid?

7. ♠ J 9 5 4	8. ♠ 5 3	9. ♠ - - -
♡ 7 4	♡ J 8 7	♡ Q 8 2
◇ 9 8 7 5 2	◇ 6 5 4 2	◇ J 9 7 6 5 4
♣ J 2	♣ 9 7 4 3	♣ 8 7 4 3

Partner opened 2♡. Your response?

10. ♠ Q 10 3	11. ♠ K J 7 5	12. ♠ K 7
♡ 8 5	♡ Q 4 2	♡ 6 2
◇ 9 7 4 2	◇ 9 8 6 2	◇ K Q 8 3 2
♣ Q 8 5 3	♣ 5 2	♣ 8 7 5 2

Answers to Exercises:

1. 2 ◇	2. 3 ♣	3. 2 NT
4. 3 ♣	5. 3 NT	6. 2 ♠
7. 4 ♠	8. 2 NT	9. 3 ◇
10. 2 NT	11. 4 ♡	12. 3 ◇

Chapter 15

Overcalls

A suit bid or a no trump bid after an opponent has opened the bidding is known as an 'overcall'. An overcall may be made with fewer points than an opening but the overcall shows a strong 5-card or longer suit. If you do not have a long, strong suit, you should pass unless your hand is worth a 1NT overcall (16-18 points) or a takeout double (see Chapter 16).

1NT overcall: 16-18 points, a balanced hand and at least one stopper in their suit. If responder has a balanced hand, pass with 0-7 points, raise to 2NT with 8-9 points and bid 3NT with 10 points or more. With an unbalanced hand, bid your long suit at the 2-level with no chance for game, bid at the 3-level with enough for game and a 5-card suit and bid 4♡/4♠ with enough for game and a 6-card or longer suit.

1-level overcall: A strong 5-card or longer suit and 8-15 HCP. As the maximum is 15 points, there is little incentive for responder to reply with 6-7 points. You may raise with just three trumps. Support to the 2-level is 8-11 points, to the 3-level 12-15 points, and with 16 points or more, you are worth a shot at game. Without support you may bid 1NT (8-11), 2NT (12-15) or 3NT (16-up) with a balanced hand and a stopper in their suit. Otherwise, you may change suit with a good suit of your own.

2-level overcall: A strong 5-card or longer suit and 10-15 HCP. Again there is little point in replying with a very weak hand. Raise to the 3-level with 10-12 points and to the 4-level with 13-15. Opposite a minor suit overcall, prefer to try for 3NT with a suitable hand. Any change of suit will be a good 5-card suit and 10 points or more.

Jump overcall, e.g. (1♣) : 2♡ or (1♠) : 3♢. A strong 6-card or longer suit and 16-18 points. With more points, start with a double. With only a 5-card suit, also start with a double. You can bid your long suit after partner's reply to your double.

EXERCISES

Your right-hand opponent opened 1 ♡. What action do you take?

1. ♠ A K J 5 2
   ♡ 9 8
   ◇ J 9 8 2
   ♣ 5 2

2. ♠ A K J
   ♡ 8 7 4 2
   ◇ K Q J
   ♣ 7 5 3

3. ♠ A K
   ♡ K 6 4
   ◇ J 8 7 4 3
   ♣ 8 3 2

4. ♠ A Q 3
   ♡ K Q 9
   ◇ A 7 4
   ♣ Q 8 3 2

5. ♠ J 7 6
   ♡ A
   ◇ Q J 8 6 4 2
   ♣ K J 2

6. ♠ Q 3
   ♡ 7 2
   ◇ A Q 2
   ♣ A K Q 9 5 2

Left-hand opponent opened 1 ◇. Partner has overcalled 1 ♠ and there is a pass on your right. What action do you take on these hands?

7. ♠ J 9 5
   ♡ 7 4 2
   ◇ A 7 5
   ♣ Q 8 6 2

8. ♠ 5 3
   ♡ Q J 8 7 3 2
   ◇ 2
   ♣ A K 4 3

9. ♠ A 9 8
   ♡ J 5 2
   ◇ 9 6
   ♣ K Q 7 6 2

10. ♠ 10 3
    ♡ Q 8 3 2
    ◇ A J 4
    ♣ K 6 4 3

11. ♠ A 9 8 6 5
    ♡ 7
    ◇ 6 4
    ♣ A K J 7 2

12. ♠ 7 5 3
    ♡ A Q 9
    ◇ K Q J 5
    ♣ K J 2

Answers to Exercises:

1. 1 ♠

2. No bid

3. No bid

4. 1 NT

5. 2 ◇

6. 3 ♣

7. No bid

8. 2 ♡

9. 2 ♠

10. 1 NT

11. 4 ♠

12. 3 NT

Chapter 16

Doubles

PENALTY DOUBLES

If the opponents bid at the 3-level or higher and you feel sure you can defeat their contract by two tricks or more, double. This double is for penalties and asks partner to pass. Your double tells partner that you wish to defend and increase the bonus score for defeating their contract.

TAKEOUT DOUBLES

At the 1-level or 2-level, a double is used for a different purpose. Penalties at these low levels are rare and so the double has become a request for partner to bid something, anything, to remove the double, to take out the double by bidding. A double of 1NT or 2NT is still used as a penalty double, but a low level double of a suit bid asks partner to reply. It is a forcing bid.

If an opponent has opened with a 1-level suit bid, you should double with 10-12 HCP and a singleton or void in their suit plus support for the other three suits: *Or* 13 HCP or more plus a doubleton, singleton or void in their suit and support for the other suits: *Or* 16-18 HCP and a long suit (double first and bid your long suit on the next round): *Or* 16-18 HCP and a balanced hand but no stopper in their suit (so that the 1NT overcall is not available): *Or* any hand with 19 or more HCP.

RESPONDING TO THE TAKEOUT DOUBLE

When replying in a suit, count HCP plus Trump Points.

0-5 points: Bid a suit, preferably a major. With both majors or both minors, bid the longer suit or if equal length, choose the stronger.

6-9 points: Bid a suit or 1NT. The 1NT bid promises a stopper in their suit and denies a major suit. With a choice of actions, majors come first, no trumps next and a minor suit bid is the last choice.

10-12 points: Jump bid in a suit or jump bid in no trumps. Again, majors come first, no trumps second choice and minors last.

13 points or more: You have enough to bid a game.

EXERCISES

Your right-hand opponent opened 1♡. What action do you take?

1. ♠ A K J 5
   ♡ 9 8
   ◊ J 9 8 2
   ♣ A 8 7

2. ♠ Q J 7 2
   ♡ - - -
   ◊ A 9 8 6
   ♣ A 9 7 5 3

3. ♠ 7
   ♡ K 6 4 3
   ◊ K Q 7 4
   ♣ A 6 5 2

4. ♠ A J 6 3
   ♡ 9 7 2
   ◊ A K J 7 4
   ♣ A

5. ♠ Q 7 6
   ♡ 9 7 2
   ◊ A Q J 6
   ♣ A K J

6. ♠ Q 3
   ♡ A 7 6
   ◊ A Q 4 2
   ♣ A K Q 9

Left-hand opponent opened 1◊. Partner has doubled and there is a pass on your right. What action do you take on these hands?

7. ♠ J 9 5 2
   ♡ 7 4
   ◊ A 7 5
   ♣ 9 8 6 2

8. ♠ 5 3
   ♡ 7 3
   ◊ 9 7 5 2
   ♣ 8 7 6 4 3

9. ♠ A 9 8
   ♡ J 5
   ◊ Q J 9 6
   ♣ 8 6 3 2

10. ♠ 10 3
    ♡ K Q 8 3
    ◊ A 8 4
    ♣ Q 6 4 3

11. ♠ A Q J 8 7 2
    ♡ 7
    ◊ 6 4
    ♣ K J 7 2

12. ♠ Q 5 2
    ♡ K 8 4
    ◊ K Q 5
    ♣ J 8 6 2

Answers to Exercises:

1. Double

2. Double

3. No bid

4. Double

5. Double

6. Double

7. 1 ♠

8. 2 ♣

9. 1 NT

10. 2 ♡

11. 4 ♠

12. 2 NT

Chapter 17

Pass Out Bidding

Suppose the bidding has started along these lines:

WEST	NORTH	EAST	SOUTH
1-of-a-suit	Pass	Pass	?

There is a great incentive for South to bid. If South passes, the bidding is over. South is said to be in the 'pass out' seat. If South does pass, West becomes declarer in a meagre 1-contract. East must have a very weak hand to pass and most of the time North-South will be able to make a contract quite comfortably.

Rather than sell out at such a low level, a player in the pass out seat is encouraged to bid on very slender values. In the pass out seat at the 1-level, actions are at least 3 points lower than the same action as a direct overcall:

1NT = 13-15 points, a balanced hand and a stopper in their suit.

2NT = 16-18 points, a balanced hand and a stopper in their suit.

Suit overcall = 7 points or more. The suit need not be a strong suit in the pass out seat. (A direct overcall is always a good suit.)

Jump overcall = 13-15 points and a good 5-card or longer suit.

Double is used for other hands worth a competitive bid. You may double in the pass out seat with:

- 7-9 points, a singleton or void in their suit, support for the other suits.
- 10-12 points and no 5-card suit worth bidding.
- 13 points or more with no strong suit and not worth 1NT or 2NT.

The double in the pass out seat is far less restricted than in second seat. Partner replies to the double in the normal fashion, as the doubler may have a strong hand. If weak, the doubler will pass the reply.

If the opponents bid and raise their suit only to the 2-level and the bidding reaches you in the pass out seat, again you should strive to bid.

EXERCISES

Your left-hand opponent opened 1 ♡, no bid from partner, no bid on your right. What action do you take in the pass out seat?

1. ♠ A Q 9 5
   ♡ 9
   ◇ J 7 5 2
   ♣ A 8 7 6

2. ♠ Q 9 8 7 2
   ♡ 7 6 2
   ◇ A 6
   ♣ K 5 3

3. ♠ 7
   ♡ K 6 4 3
   ◇ K Q
   ♣ J 8 7 6 5 2

4. ♠ J 5 4
   ♡ 9 7 2
   ◇ A K J 7 6 4
   ♣ A

5. ♠ K 7 6
   ♡ K 7 2
   ◇ A J 5
   ♣ Q 8 7 2

6. ♠ A 3
   ♡ A J 6
   ◇ A Q 4 2
   ♣ Q 9 6 2

7. ♠ A 9 5
   ♡ 7 4
   ◇ A Q 7 5
   ♣ 9 8 6 2

8. ♠ 9 6 5 2
   ♡ - - -
   ◇ A J 5 2
   ♣ A 7 6 4 3

9. ♠ A K 8 2
   ♡ J 5
   ◇ A Q J 9 6
   ♣ Q 6

Right-hand opponent opened 1 ♡, no bid by you, 2 ♡ on your left, no bid from partner, no bid on your right. What action do you take on these hands?

10. ♠ 10 8 7 5 3 2
    ♡ A 8
    ◇ A
    ♣ 7 6 4 3

11. ♠ Q J 8 7
    ♡ 7
    ◇ K 9 7 4
    ♣ K J 8 5

12. ♠ 5 2
    ♡ K 8 4
    ◇ 8 5
    ♣ K Q 9 7 5 4

Answers to Exercises:

1. Double

2. 1 ♠

3. 2 ♣

4. 3 ◇

5. 1 NT

6. 2 NT

7. Double

8. Double

9. Double

10. 2 ♠

11. Double

12. 3 ♣

Chapter 18

Bidding Tips

● If partner has shown a hand with no singleton, no void, you have a sound trump fit when you hold a 6-card or longer suit. Suppose partner has opened 1NT and you hold six spades. Partner is bound to hold at least two spades, so that you have at least eight spades together. This is important because it allows you to count shortage points.

♠ K 10 9 7 6 2   Suppose you hold these cards and partner has
♡ - - -   opened 1NT. Your best action is 4♠. You know
♢ A J 3 2   partner has at least two spades, so your hand is
♣ 9 3 2   worth 13 points, counting the void.

You can rely on partner having no singleton, no void if partner opens 1NT, 2NT or 3NT or partner responds 2NT or 3NT or opener's first rebid is 2NT or 3NT. A 1NT response or a 1NT rebid is occasionally made with a singleton in partner's suit if no other action is suitable.

● If either player bids a higher suit followed by a lower suit, this will promise at least five cards in the first suit. If each suit had four cards, the cheaper suit would have been bid first.

WEST	EAST	West will have at least 5 hearts-4 clubs.
1♡	1♠	With 4 hearts and 4 clubs, West would have
2♣		opened 1♣. East can support hearts with 3.

WEST	EAST	East has shown at least five spades and four
1♣	1♠	diamonds. With two 4-card suits, East would
2♣	2♢	have responded 1♢ first. West can now
?		support spades with 3-card support.

● Opener is showing 16-18 points if opener makes a jump rebid in a bid suit, such as 1♢ : 1♠, 3♢ or 1♢ : 1♠, 3♠. Opener shows 16 or more points if opener changes suit to the 3-level (for example, 1♠ : 2♢, 3♣). With a weaker hand, stay at the 2-level. A jump shift by opener such as 1♢ : 1♠, 3♣ shows 19 points or better and is forcing to game.

EXERCISES

Partner opened 1NT. What is your response?

1. ♠ Q 9 5
   ♡ 9 7 6 5 4 3 2
   ♦ 4
   ♣ J 7

2. ♠ K J 8 7 4 2
   ♡ A Q 2
   ♦ A 6 2
   ♣ 3

3. ♠ - - -
   ♡ J 8 7 5 4 3 2
   ♦ A K Q
   ♣ 9 5 2

Partner: 1♡, you: 1♠, partner: 2♣. Your rebid?

4. ♠ A Q 9 5
   ♡ 7 4 2
   ♦ J 6 3
   ♣ 8 7 4

5. ♠ J 9 6 5 2
   ♡ A 9 8
   ♦ A 7
   ♣ J 6 4

6. ♠ A K 8 6 2
   ♡ Q J 5
   ♦ A 6
   ♣ 9 6 5

You: 1♣, partner: 1♠, you: 2♣, partner: 2♡. Your rebid?

7. ♠ J 5 4
   ♡ Q 7 6
   ♦ 7
   ♣ A K Q 9 7 2

8. ♠ A 7
   ♡ K 8
   ♦ J 8 5
   ♣ K Q 7 4 3 2

9. ♠ 8 2
   ♡ 7 4
   ♦ A Q 2
   ♣ A K 9 6 4 3

You opened 1♠ and partner replied 2♡. Your rebid?

10. ♠ A K 7 5 3
    ♡ A
    ♦ A Q 6 2
    ♣ 8 4 3

11. ♠ K Q 5 4 2
    ♡ 8
    ♦ A Q 6 2
    ♣ J 5 3

12. ♠ Q J 7 5 2
    ♡ 4
    ♦ A K 9 6 3
    ♣ Q 9

Answers to Exercises:

1. 2 ♡

2. 4 ♠

3. 4 ♡

4. 2 ♡

5. 3 ♡

6. 4 ♡

7. 2 ♠

8. 2 ♠

9. 2 NT

10. 3 ♦

11. 2 ♠

12. 2 ♠

Chapter 19

Competitive Bidding

You will find that the opponents often bid after your side has opened the bidding. This may make it awkward for you as responder or for your rebid as opener. If their interference does not prevent your normal bid, make your normal bid. If you have a clearcut bid, make it. If you have a minimum hand and nothing special to say, you should pass. Partner can still bid again if partner wishes to compete. In the meantime, your pass indicates that you have nothing very worthwhile.

As responder needs at least 10 points for a new suit reply at the 2-level, and opener needs 16 points or more to bid a new suit at the 3-level, you can sometimes be stuck for a bid with quite a decent hand. Both opener and responder can use a takeout double to solve such problems.

A double at the 1-level or 2-level asks partner to bid. It is a takeout double and will be shortish in the enemy suit.

A double at the 3-level or higher asks partner to pass. This penalty double is used when you believe the opponents will fail in their contract and you want to score higher bonus points for defeating them. This usually happens when you are strong in their suit.

At the 1-level or 2-level, it is rare to have enough to score a large penalty. That is why the double is useful to ask partner to bid something.

♠ A J 7 3   Suppose partner opens 1♡ and the next player
♡ Q 6   overcalls 2◇. After a pass, you would have bid 1♠
◇ 8 7   (not good enough for 2♣) but you are not strong
♣ J 9 6 5 4   enough for 2♠ or 3♣. Yet you are worth action.
After all, your side has more than 20 points. What should you do? The best call is 'Double'. This tells partner you have enough to reply but no clearcut action. Whatever partner now bids will suit you.

♠ J 8 6   Suppose you opened 1♣, partner responded 1♠
♡ 6   and the next player bid 2♡. What action should
◇ A K 5 3   you take? Again, best is to double. This suggests
♣ A Q 9 7 2   shortage in hearts and support for the other suits.

EXERCISES

Partner opened 1♠, right-hand opponent bid 2♣. Your action?

1. ♠ J 5
   ♡ K J 9 8
   ◇ Q 9 8 2
   ♣ 6 3 2

2. ♠ 7 2
   ♡ K J 8 7 3 2
   ◇ A 9
   ♣ 7 4 3

3. ♠ 7 2
   ♡ K J 8 7 3 2
   ◇ A Q
   ♣ 7 4 3

4. ♠ 6 3
   ♡ 9 7
   ◇ A Q 8 7 4 2
   ♣ 9 5 2

5. ♠ 7 6
   ♡ 9 7
   ◇ A Q 8 7 4 2
   ♣ A J 4

6. ♠ K 3
   ♡ A Q 6
   ◇ A K J 8 7 2
   ♣ 8 3

You opened 1◇, partner responded 1♠ and right-hand opponent bid 2♡. What action do you take on these hands?

7. ♠ J 9 5 2
   ♡ 7 4
   ◇ A K J 7 5
   ♣ K 2

8. ♠ K 5 3
   ♡ 7
   ◇ A K J 5 2
   ♣ Q 6 4 3

9. ♠ 9 8
   ♡ A 5
   ◇ A 8 7 4 3
   ♣ A 6 3 2

10. ♠ K 3
    ♡ 3
    ◇ A Q 9 8 4
    ♣ A K J 7 3

11. ♠ A J 8
    ♡ 7 5
    ◇ A Q 6 4 2
    ♣ K Q 7

12. ♠ 7 5
    ♡ K 8
    ◇ K Q J 5 3 2
    ♣ A K 2

Answers to Exercises:

1. Double

2. Double

3. 2 ♡

4. Pass

5. 2 ◇

6. 3 ◇

7. 2 ♠

8. Double

9. Pass

10. 3 ♣

11. Double

12. 3 ◇

Chapter 20

Pre-emptive Bids

You and partner score points by bidding accurately to your best contract and making it. You can also do well by preventing the opponents finding their best contract. By striking the first blow, by bidding to a high level before they have a chance to bid, you may win the bidding at little cost or you may make it too difficult for them to locate their best spot. That is the object of pre-emptive bidding.

PRE-EMPTIVE OPENINGS
These are opening bids at the 3-level or higher. With the bidding starting at a high level, the opponents will be unable to exchange accurate information about their hands. Forced to guess, they will often end in the wrong contract. They may stop in game when they belong in slam. They may end up in the wrong game.

You may open with a pre-empt with a 7-card or longer suit and about 6-9 HCP. These openings are always based on weak points. With a strong hand, there is no need to try to shut them out. Try to estimate how many tricks you are likely to win if your suit is trumps. If not vulnerable, open 3 of your suit with 6 tricks, 4 of your suit with 7 tricks and 5♣ or 5♢ with a long minor and 8 tricks. If your side is vulnerable, you should hold one trick more: 7 tricks for a 3-opening, 8 tricks for a 4-opening and 9 tricks to open 5♣ or 5♢.

PRE-EMPTIVE RAISES
The raise of opener's suit to the 4-level (such as 1♠ : 4♠) is often used to shut out fourth player. The shut-out raise shows five trumps or more, an unbalanced hand and under 10 HCP.

PRE-EMPTIVE OVERCALLS
You can also use a shut-out bid after an opponent has opened. A pre-emptive overcall skips at least two levels of bidding, such as (1♣) : 3♡. Again, the hand should hold at least a good 7-card suit and not too much in the way of high cards. The number of tricks which you should win if your suit is trumps is the same as for the pre-emptive openings. Note that bids like (1♠) : 3♢ are not pre-emptive bids as this skips over only one level (2♢). To qualify as a pre-empt, the bid must jump at least two levels of bidding.

Chapter 21

Passed Hand Bidding

Once you have passed initially, the meaning of some of your bids will be affected. You cannot hold 13 points or more, else you would have opened, and even 12 HCP is unlikely. Your no trump responses (1NT 6-9, 2NT 10-12) are not affected as they show less than 13 HCP even when you have not passed. Similarly, raising opener's suit (to the 2-level with 6-9 and to the 3-level with 10-12) remains unaffected.

A change of suit at the 1-level shows 6-12 points rather than the usual 6-15 points. It is a 4-card or longer suit, as normal. The new suit by a passed hand is not forcing.

A change of suit at the 2-level has a range of 10-12 points rather then the usual 10-15. A difference, however, is that a new suit at the 2-level by a passed hand shows a 5-card or longer suit. Without a long suit, bid at the 1-level or respond 1NT or 2NT or raise opener's suit. The new suit at the 2-level by a passed hand is not forcing. Opener should be prepared to pass it with a minimum opening and doubleton or better support.

A jump shift by a passed hand (e.g. Pass : 1 ◇, 2♠) shows 10-12 points and a strong 5-card suit. If the suit is only four cards long or if the suit is not strong, bid the suit at the cheapest level without a jump.

The most important rule about bidding by a passed hand is:

A BID BY A PASSED HAND IS NOT FORCING

This applies whether it is a jump shift or a change of suit. The normal rules about change-of-suit-forcing or the jump shift forcing to game do not apply when responder is a passed hand. Because any bid by a passed hand can be passed by opener, it is vital to make a response which gives partner the most important information in one bid – there might be no second chance. Therefore, raise a major suit as first priority. Do not change suit when you have a major suit raise available. Otherwise, you might be passed out in an inferior contract.

Chapter 22

Leads And Signals

THE CARD TO LEAD IN A TRUMP CONTRACT

With 2 or more touching honours, lead top of the touching cards: Ace from A-K suits, K from K-Q, Q from Q-J, J from J-10, 10 from 10-9.

Without touching honours:
1. Lead top from a doubleton (K from K-5, 8 from 8-3, 3 from 3-2).
2. Lead bottom from a 3-card suit with an honour (4 from Q-7-4).
3. Lead middle from a 3-card suit with an honour (5 from 8-5-2).
4. Lead 4th highest from 4-card or longer suits (5 from K-J-8-5-3).

THE CARD TO LEAD IN NO TRUMPS

Exactly the same as above except to lead top of touching cards in a long suit you need three honour cards, not just two. With only two honours in a 4-card or longer suit, lead 4th highest. Thus, you lead the Q from Q-J-10-6-4, but the 6 from Q-J-7-6-4. From K-J-10-7-3, you lead the jack – you have three honours in the suit.

From 3-card suits you still lead top of two touching honours. Lead top from K-Q-3, Q-J-5, J-10-5, 10-9-2.

SIGNALS WHEN FOLLOWING TO PARTNER'S LEAD

If you cannot win the trick, you can still signal to partner whether you like partner's lead. If you want the suit continued, play the highest card you can afford. If you want a switch, play your lowest card.

High card = 'I like this suit. Please keep playing it.'
Lowest card = 'I do not like this suit. Please try something else.'

SIGNALS WHEN DISCARDING

Discard the lowest card in the suit you do not want partner to play. When partner sees you discard the lowest card, partner knows you do not want that suit led. A high discard asks partner to play that suit but very often you cannot afford to discard a high card in a valuable suit.

Chapter 23

Tips On Card Play

Bidding accurately to the best contract is half your problem. The other half is making your contract. It is no good being in the best spot if your card play lets you down. It is worthwhile becoming a good declarer or a good defender since you then win more points through your skilful play.

Once a player's enthusiasm to improve is aroused, there are many excellent books devoted just to card play at bridge. This chapter contains useful advice on playing your cards to best advantage.

YOU ARE DECLARER IN A TRUMP CONTRACT
Draw Trumps

On most hands it pays you to eliminate trumps held by the opponents. If you allow them to keep their trumps, they can ruff your winning cards when they run out of that suit. If you have removed their trumps, your winners in the other suits cannot be beaten.

In most trump contracts, you will have more trumps than the opponents do. If you have 8 trumps, they have 5. If you have 9 trumps, they have 4. As you play each round of trumps, count their trumps as they fall. If they began with 5 and they played one each, they still hold 3 trumps. If you play another round and both opponents follow, there is just one trump missing. If their last trump is lower than yours, remove it. If their last trump is higher than yours, leave it out. It will take a trick sooner or later and there is no reason why you should lose two trumps to their one and give them the lead when it is not necessary.

After trumps have been drawn, play your next strongest suit. If you have a suit with high cards missing the ace or king, tackle that next. For example, with K-Q-J opposite 7-5-2, you can set up two winners by forcing out their ace. If you have a second suit with 7 or more cards, you have more cards in this suit than they do. Keep on with this suit and when they run out, your remaining cards in the suit are winners.

If you hold only 7 trumps between you and dummy, or even fewer, it is often best not to draw trumps. The opponents have almost as many trumps as you do. A better move is to try to win tricks with your low trumps by ruffing. Also if dummy has a short suit and not many trumps, it is usually best to play dummy's short suit first, ruff your losers in dummy and draw trumps later. Each time you ruff a loser in dummy, you have won an extra trick.

DECLARER PLAY IN NO TRUMPS

You should start by counting your certain winners in dummy and in your own hand. If you have enough for your contract, you can just play out your winners. This would be rare and most of the time you will need to set up 1, 2 or more extra tricks. If so, set up those extra tricks first and do not play your sure winners yet. Those winners allow you to win the lead later on, they are your 'entries' to play out your other winners.

Setting up extra tricks may involve forcing out high cards held by the opponents. If you have K-Q-J-10 opposite 5-4-2, there are three tricks available, but only after you have forced out their ace. If you hold Q-J-10-9 with no high cards opposite, you can still set up two extra tricks by forcing out their ace and their king. You will have to lose the lead twice and that is why you need those winners in your other suits, so that you can win the lead again later.

You can also build up extra tricks when you have more cards in a suit than the opponents. If you hold A-9-5-3-2 opposite K-7-6-4, you have 9 cards, they have 4. If they both follow twice when you play ace and king, their cards in the suit have gone and your low cards are now all winners. If one opponent shows out on the second round, there is still one card left in the suit. Play the suit again and force out their high card. You will lose the lead (so what?) but you will set up two extra tricks.

Even with no high cards, you may be able to set up extra tricks. If you hold 9-6-5-3 opposite 8-7-4-2 and play this suit at each opportunity, you can set up one extra trick if the high cards held by the opponents are divided 3-2. The key to no trumps is playing those suits which can bring you extra tricks. Do not worry about losing the lead.

THE OPENING LEAD IN NO TRUMPS

Lead your partner's suit if partner has bid. If partner has not bid, lead your own best suit, usually your longest suit which the opponents have not bid. It is not a good idea to lead a suit which the opponents have bid. You would be helping them to set up tricks in their suit.

With two equally long suits, prefer the stronger suit. Sometimes you may have a strong 4-card suit and a weaker 5-card suit (such as K-Q-J-10 versus J-7-4-3-2). If the 4-card suit has three honour cards, choose that lead; otherwise stick with the longer suit.

THE OPENING LEAD IN A TRUMP CONTRACT

Prefer to lead partner's suit. Next choice, an unbid suit. Stay away from a suit bid by the opposition. Usually you will be helping them if you lead their suits. However, with no good suit to lead, you can lead a trump if you hold two or three worthless trumps. This will not cost you a trick and will reduce declarer's chances for ruffing.

The basic order of preference for leads against a trump contract is:

1. Lead partner's suit.
2. Lead a 3-card or stronger sequence (such as K-Q-J-x, Q-J-10-x-x).
3. Lead a suit headed by A-K or lower touching honours.
4. Lead a singleton or a worthless doubleton. A short suit lead is best from a very weak hand. The weaker your hand, the more likely it is that partner can obtain the lead quickly and give you a ruff.
5. With none of the above, lead a suit with no honour cards.

Try to stay away from these leads, all of which are risky:

1. Leading a suit with the ace but not the king. If you must lead the suit, then lead the ace, not a low one (at least you will win one trick), but prefer not to lead the suit at all. Often this lead sets up the king or queen for declarer. Keep your aces to capture declarer's honours later.
2. Leading doubleton honours (such as K-x, Q-x, J-x, 10-x) unless partner bid the suit.
3. Leading a suit with just one honour (such as J-x-x-x or Q-x-x), unless partner had bid the suit.

THE LATER DEFENCE
RETURN PARTNER'S LEAD

This is a sensible guide. In no trumps, partner has probably led the longest suit for your side. By continuing the suit, you will help set up winners for partner. In a trump contract partner may have led a singleton and will be able to ruff if you return the suit. However, if you can tell it would be futile to return partner's suit, try some other suit.

WIN A TRICK AS CHEAPLY AS POSSIBLE

A defender wins a trick with the cheapest card possible. If you could win with the ace, king or queen, win with the queen. This helps partner work out what you have. If you win with the ace, partner knows you do not have the king. If you win with the king, you do not hold the queen.

SECOND HAND LOW

If you cannot win the trick in second seat, play a low card. If you can win the trick, it is still correct most of the time to play low to give partner a chance to win the trick. If partner cannot win the trick, then win it yourself. If you defeat the contract by winning the trick, take it – do not leave it to partner. If you can win the trick in second seat, and this may be your only chance to win a trick with this high card, grab the trick. If you are not sure, it is better to win the trick.

COVER AN HONOUR WITH AN HONOUR

If declarer leads an honour card from hand or from dummy, play a higher honour in second seat if it will help you to win an extra trick in that suit or if it might help to build up extra winners for partner. Do not cover an honour with an honour if you know that partner holds a singleton or a doubleton in the suit and you cannot build up any extra trick for yourself by covering.

OBEY PARTNER'S SIGNALS

You should feel obliged to obey signals from your partner (see Chapter 22), unless you can tell that it would be wrong. If partner asks for a suit, lead it. If partner's signal says, 'Do not play this suit', then do not play it (unless you are right to disobey!).

KEEP LENGTH WITH DUMMY

If dummy has a 4-card or longer suit and you hold 4 or more cards in that suit, do not discard from that suit if you can beat one of dummy's cards. This will limit declarer's tricks in that suit.

THIRD HAND HIGH

If dummy has only low cards, play high in third seat if partner's card is not going to win the trick.

	DUMMY			DUMMY	
	7 5 3			7 5 3	
WEST		EAST	WEST		EAST
Q J 10 9 2		A 8 6 4	Q J 6 2		K 9 4
	K			A 10 8	

West leads the queen. East should play the ace. This prevents South winning an undeserved trick. From the Q lead, East knows South has the king. As the queen will not win, play your ace. If the king did not fall under the ace, you can still continue the suit.

Even if you cannot win the trick in 3rd seat, you should play high. You may build up winners for partner. West leads the 2. East should play the king. This sets up West's queen and jack as winners and stops South winning a second trick with the 10.

When playing 3rd-hand-high with equally high cards, play the cheapest of equal cards. If partner and dummy play low and you hold K-Q-J-5 in third seat, play the jack, your cheapest high card. This is part of the rule which says a defender should win or try to win as cheaply as possible.

If dummy has a high card and 3rd player has that high card surrounded, play the lower surrounding card if dummy plays low. For example:

	DUMMY			DUMMY	
	Q 8 3			J 5 3	
WEST		EAST	WEST		EAST
10 7 4 2		K J 9	K 6 2		Q 10 9 7
	A 6 5			A 8 4	

West leads the 2 and dummy plays low. East's K-J surround the Q. East should play the jack.

West leads the 2 and dummy plays low. East's Q-10-9 surround the jack. East should play the 9.

Chapter 24

How To Improve

After your child has learnt how to play and has been playing for some time, there are several ways improvement is possible.

1. Try to play as often as possible. The more often you play, the quicker the learning. You need to balance bridge against other important activities (such as homework, studies, outdoor games).

2. If your child is playing reasonably, invite others to join you for a friendly game. Another adult-child partnership would make a good challenge. Once a reasonable standard has been reached, you could invite one or two stronger players. They should not be so strong that your child is out of his depth. Always make sure that the players invited are pleasant, congenial and good-natured. You should warn them in advance that you are just starting on bridge.

3. Spend a little time with your child watching the top players in action. Your local club will let you know when they play and it costs you nothing to go along and watch how the experts play.

4. Read some more bridge books, particularly on declarer play and defence. Here are some suggestions:
BASIC BRIDGE: A Guide to Good Acol Bidding and Play
GUIDE TO BETTER ACOL BRIDGE
The Mini-Master series of inexpensive booklets on bidding and play published in the *Master Bridge Series*. (List of titles available from Victor Gollancz Ltd, 14 Henrietta Street, London WC2E 8QJ)
A subscription to a bridge magazine makes a nice present.

5. A course of lessons with the best teachers available is worthwhile when your child wishes to move on to more advanced methods.

Chapter 25

The Young, Young World Of Bridge

Thirty years ago the young world champions were usually players in their forties. Today they are more likely to be in their twenties. When the United States won the Bermuda Bowl (the World Teams Championship) in 1981, the team included Jeff Meckstroth aged 25, Eric Rodwell just turned 24, and the youngest player ever to win the Bermuda Bowl, Bobby Levin was 23. Meckstroth and Rodwell went on to win the World Pairs convincingly in 1986 and were part of the USA team that won the World Open Teams Olympiad in 1988.

The Danish Women's Team that won the 1988 Women's Teams Olympiad included Bettina Kalkerup, aged 25, and Charlotte Palmund, who was 23. The same pair two years earlier had finished second in the Women's World Pairs Championship at their first appearance in a world championship.

Most countries run masterpoint schemes where tournament players earn awards for performing well in tournament play. The largest such scheme is conducted by the U.S.A. with around 200,000 registered players. The highest award in the U.S.A. is Life Master, a status not achieved by most players. The youngest players in the US to become Life Masters are pre-teens. For many years the record has been held by Douglas Hsieh who became a Life Master at the age of 11 years, 10 months, 4 days. In 1988 this was bettered by Sam Hirschman who became a Life Master at 11 years, 9 months, 5 days.

Many countries conduct competitions restricted to young players. The U.S.A. has a King/Queen of Bridge award recognising achievement in the bridge world by high school students. Like many other countries, the U.S.A. conducts an annual intervarsity championship.

Europe has conducted European Youth Championships for many years and 1988 saw the first Far East Junior Teams Championship.

The World Bridge Federation has instituted the World Junior Championships, restricted to players under 25 on 1st January or aged 25 if winners of a zonal junior championship. These championships are to be held every two years in odd-numbered years.

The 2nd World Championship in 1989, held in England, was won by Great Britain who defeated Argentina in the final. France came third, Australia fourth, followed by Indonesia, North America, Central America and India. The 1st World Junior Championship in 1987 was won by Holland, the reigning European junior champions. Holland defeated France in the final, with the U.S.A. third. Other teams competing were Argentina and Indonesia.

Holland's victory came as no surprise as Holland leads the world with its youth bridge programme, in and out of schools. The 7th European Bridge Camp, a biennial summer event, was also held in Holland in 1987, with almost 100 young players from 12 countries competing in teams and pairs events as well as attending bridge seminars during the 8-day camp.

In view of the above, perhaps this hand will not come as such a surprise:

Dealer East: North-South vulnerable

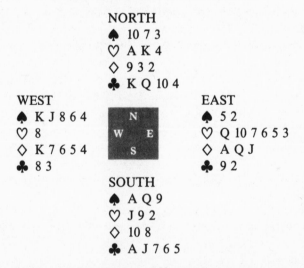

NORTH
♠ 10 7 3
♡ A K 4
◇ 9 3 2
♣ K Q 10 4

WEST
♠ K J 8 6 4
♡ 8
◇ K 7 6 5 4
♣ 8 3

EAST
♠ 5 2
♡ Q 10 7 6 5 3
◇ A Q J
♣ 9 2

SOUTH
♠ A Q 9
♡ J 9 2
◇ 10 8
♣ A J 7 6 5

East dealt and opened a weak 2♡. South became declarer in 3♣. West led the 8 of hearts and declarer won dummy's ace. He drew trumps in two rounds and then led a diamond from dummy.

The deal comes from the 1987 EPSON Worldwide Bridge Contest. In the souvenir booklet, Omar Sharif's analysis stated that the contract will succeed if 'East puts up the ◇A and makes the mistake of continuing diamonds instead of pushing a spade through'.

Declarer in fact demonstrated that the contract was certain to make, as long as East held the six hearts advertised by the 2♡ opening. East did win the diamond and did lead a spade through. Declarer played low and West won. A second diamond was led to East and another spade came back. This time declarer won the ace, crossed to dummy with a trump and ruffed dummy's last diamond. Now he played a spade.

When West won the trick, a spade or a diamond had to come back. This gave declarer a ruff and discard and allowed South to get rid of his heart loser. Had East won the third round of spades, either a ruff and discard would again be conceded or a heart lead would be won by declarer's jack. As long as East held six hearts originally, the defence was stymied.

This is more than just a well-played hand. There were 70,000 competitors in the 1987 EPSON and this was judged the Best Played Hand. Sitting North was 19-year-old Tom Puczynski of Warsaw, Poland, while South, the successful declarer, was his brother Mariusz. Age? 17 years!

It certainly is a young, young world of bridge.

Appendix 1

Bridge For Two Or Three Players

When you are short of a player or two for a regular game of bridge, try one of these variations which are suitable for two or three players.

BRIDGE FOR TWO

1. *Bidding practice:* Remove any 20 low cards from the pack. Deal 13 cards to each of you and bid the hands. It is a good idea to write down your bidding so that you can go over it later. This is an excellent way to practise your slam bidding since the hands will have enough for a game, a small slam or a grand slam. After you have finished bidding, reveal the cards and check whether you are in a good contract. If not, go over the bidding to see how you might have done better.

2. Deal out 4 hands as usual. Turn 7 cards face up in the hand opposite each player. You can now see your own 13 cards plus the 7 in your 'dummy'. Bid against each other. When the bidding ends, a card is led as normal. The rest of declarer's dummy is revealed and the other dummy is concealed again. Declarer plays as normal, the defender plays alternately from the other two hands. The scoring is standard and you play one rubber at a time.

BRIDGE FOR THREE

1. Deal out 4 hands of 13 cards. There is no bidding. Each player in turn is the declarer and the spare hand is the dummy. The contract is always 2NT doubled. The player on the left of declarer leads, then dummy is revealed and play proceeds as normal. After play is over, the hand is scored up. Each declarer is playing a separate rubber. When one declarer's rubber is over, continue with the remaining rubbers until all 3 rubbers are finished. Then tally each player's score. This game is good fun and is an excellent way of practising declarer play and defence. It also teaches the scoring for doubled contracts.

2. Deal out 4 hands of 13 cards. Turn 7 cards face up in the spare hand. Each of the three players bids against the others for the right to be declarer. You judge your bidding by your own cards plus what you can see so far in the dummy. After the first round of bidding, another card is turned up in the dummy. After the next round, another card is turned up. After two players pass, the bidding is over. The player on the left of declarer leads a card, the rest of dummy is revealed and play continues as normal. For the scoring, three separate rubbers are used, one for each player when declarer.

3. Deal out 4 hands of 13 cards. Each player calls out his high card points. Add up these points and deduct the total from 40 to find out how many HCP are in the spare hand. The player with most points is the declarer and receives as dummy the hand with the second highest HCP total. If this is a player's hand, that player gives up his hand as dummy and picks up the spare hand. In the case of a tie, the player closest to the dealer becomes the declarer. In the case of a tie for second highest HCP total, if one of the hands is the spare hand, it is the dummy. If it is one of the player's hands, the hand nearest declarer becomes the dummy and that player picks up the spare hand.

The declarer studies the dummy without showing the other players and declares a contract. If declarer and dummy hold 26 HCP or more, the contract must be 3NT or higher. If 33 HCP or more, the contract must be at least a small slam. After the contract is known, the player on declarer's left leads, then dummy is revealed and play proceeds as normal. Again, the scoring takes place over three rubbers, one for each player as declarer.

4. *Dummy Whist For Three* and *Contract Whist For Three* are also good games. See pages 39 and 41.

Appendix 2

Glossary Of Bridge Terms

Balanced	A hand pattern of 4-3-3-3, 4-4-3-2 or 5-3-3-2
Cash	To lead a winning card
Cheapest first	The order in which 4-card suits are bid
Convention	An artificial bid
Doubleton	A suit consisting of exactly two cards
Duplicate	Tournament bridge
Forcing bid	A bid that requires partner to make a bid in reply
Game force	A bid that requires the bidding to continue to game
Honour card	An ace, king, queen, jack or ten
Jump shift	A bid in a new suit that skips one level of bidding
Length points	Points counted for each card in a suit over four
Opening bid	The first bid in any auction (excluding any pass)
Opening lead	The first card played on the first trick
Overcall	A bid after the opponents have opened the bidding
Pass out seat	Bidding position after a bid and two passes
Penalty double	A double asking partner to pass and defend
Pre-emptive bid	Intended to shut the opponents out of the bidding
Renege/Revoke	Failure to follow suit when able to do so
Ruff	To play a trump card when not following suit (to trump)
Shortage points	Points counted for short suits after agreeing on trumps
Shut-out bid	Same as pre-emptive bid
Sign-off bid	Intended by the bidder to end the auction
Singleton	A holding of exactly one card in a suit
Sluff	Slang, meaning to discard (e.g. ruff-and-sluff)
Takeout double	A double asking partner to bid and remove the double
Trump Points	Same as Shortage Points
Unbalanced	Any hand pattern which includes a void or a singleton
Up-the-line	Same as 'cheapest first'
Void	Holding no cards in a suit
Vulnerable	Having won one game